CALMING THE EMOTIONAL STORM

MIND YOUR MIND

Focus On Staying Grounded For Peace And Stability

Joann Mitchell

Table of Contents

Chapter 1: 3 Ways To Calm The Emotional Storm Within You 6

Chapter 2: 6 Ways To Master Your Emotions 10

Chapter 3: 7 Ways To Cultivate Emotions That Will Lead You To Greatness 15

Chapter 4: 6 Concerning Effects of Mood On Your Life 20

Chapter 5: *5 Scientific Tricks To Become Perfectly Happy* 24

Chapter 6: 7 EASY WAYS TO BE MINDFUL EVERY DAY 28

Chapter 7: *7 Ways To Attract Happiness* 31

Chapter 8: 6 Ways To Attract Your Potential 35

Chapter 9: 7 Ways To Stop Overthinking And Relieve Stress 39

Chapter 10: 7 Reasons Why Comparison is The Thief of Joy 43

Chapter 11: Seven Habits of Mentally Strong People 47

Chapter 12: 6 Ways To Define What Is Important In Your Life 52

Chapter 13: 7 Ways To Know When It's Time To Say Goodbye To The Past 56

Chapter 14: *Five Habits For A Beautiful Life* 60

Chapter 15: 6 Ways To Achieve Peak Performance 64

Chapter 16: *7 Signs You're More Attractive Than You Think* 68

Chapter 17: *6 Ways To Deal With Betrayal* 73

Chapter 18: *6 Ways To Get People To Like You* 77

Chapter 19: 3 Steps To Choose Mind Over Mood 81

Chapter 20: *6 Signs You Need To Give Yourself Some Personal Space* 85

Chapter 21: *7 Ways To Live Together In Harmony With Your Partner* 88

Chapter 22: 6 Reasons Your Emotions Are Getting In The Way Of Your Success 92

Chapter 23: *6 Relationship Goals To Have* 97

Chapter 24: 6 Signs You Are Emotionally Unavailable 101

Chapter 25: 3 Ways To Master Your Next Move 104

Chapter 26: 6 Signs You Have A Fear of Intimacy 107
Chapter 27: 5 Habits For An Extremely Productive Day 111
Chapter 28: *7 Signs Of An Incompatible Relationship* 114

Chapter 1:
3 Ways To Calm The Emotional Storm Within You

When emotions are already intense, it's often hard to think about what you can do to help yourself, so the first thing you need to work on is getting re-regulated as quickly as possible. Here are some fast-acting skills that work by changing your body's chemistry; it will be most helpful if you first try these before you're in an emotional situation, so you know how to use them.

1. Do a forward bend

This is my favourite re-regulating skill. Bend over as though you're trying to touch your toes (it doesn't matter if you can actually touch your toes; you can also do this sitting down if you need to, by sticking your head between your knees). Take some slow, deep breaths, and hang out there for a little while (30 to 60 seconds if you can). Doing a forward bend actually activates our parasympathetic nervous system – our 'rest and digest' system – which helps us slow down and feel a little calmer. When you're ready to stand up again, just don't do it too quickly – you don't want to fall over.

2. Focus on your exhale with 'paced breathing'

It might sound like a cliché but breathing truly is one of the best ways to get your emotions to a more manageable level. In particular, focus on making your exhale longer than your inhale – this also activates our parasympathetic nervous system, again helping us feel a little calmer and getting those emotions back to a more manageable level. When you inhale, count in your head to see how long your inhale is; as you exhale, count at the same pace, ensuring your exhale is at least a little bit longer than your inhale. For example, if you get to 4 when you inhale, make sure you exhale to at least 5. For a double whammy, do this breathing while doing your forward bend.

These re-regulating skills will help you to think a little more clearly for a few minutes, but your emotions will start to intensify once more if nothing else has changed in your environment – so the next steps are needed too.

3. Increase awareness of your emotions

In order to manage emotions more effectively in the long run, you need to be more aware of your emotions and of all their components; and you need to learn to name your emotions accurately. This might sound strange – of course you know what you're feeling, right? But how do you know if what you've always called 'anger' is actually anger, and not anxiety? Most of us have never really given our emotions much thought, we just assume that what we think we feel is what we actually feel – just like we assume the colour we've always called 'blue' is actually blue; but how do we really know?

Sensitive people who have grown up in a pervasively invalidating environment often learn to ignore or not trust their emotional experiences, and try to avoid or escape those experiences, which contributes to difficulties naming emotions accurately. Indeed, anyone prone to emotion dysregulation can have trouble figuring out what they're feeling, and so walks around in an emotional 'fog'. When you're feeling 'upset', 'bad' or 'off', are you able to identify what emotion you're actually feeling? If you struggle with this, consider each of the following questions the next time you experience even a mild emotion:

- What was the prompting event or trigger for the feeling? What were you reacting to? (Don't judge whether your response was right or wrong, just be descriptive.)

- What were your thoughts about the situation? How did you interpret what was happening? Did you notice yourself judging, jumping to conclusions, or making assumptions?

- What did you notice in your body? For example, tension or tightness in certain areas? Changes in your breathing, your heart rate, your temperature?

- What was your body doing? Describe your body language, posture and facial expression.

- What urges were you noticing? Did you want to yell or throw things? Was the urge to not make eye contact, to avoid or escape a situation you were in?

- What were your actions? Did you act on any of the urges you noted above? Did you do something else instead?

Going through this exercise will help you increase your ability to name your emotions accurately. Once you've asked yourself the above questions, you could try asking yourself if your emotion fits into one of these four (almost rhyming) categories: mad, sad, glad, and afraid. These are terms I use with clients as a helpful starting point for distinguishing basic emotions, but gradually you can work on getting more specific; emotions lists can also be helpful.

Chapter 2:
6 Ways To Master Your Emotions

As reported by Psychology Today, psychology's answer to the question of "What is emotional mastery?" Has evolved over the last century. Early American psychology embraced the "James-Lange Theory," which held that emotions are strictly the product of physiology (a neurological response to some external stimuli). This view evolved when the "Cannon-Bard Theory" asserted that the brain's thalamus mediates between external stimuli and subjective emotional experience.

The concept of emotional mastery wasn't introduced until the 1960s with the Schachter-Singer experiment, where researchers gave participants a dose of a placebo "vitamin." Participants then watched colleagues complete a set of questionnaires. When the colleagues responded angrily to the questionnaires, the participants felt angry in turn. But when the colleagues responded happily, the participants also felt happy. The study's results implied a connection between peer influence and the felt experience of emotion.

The idea that emotions are influenced by outer as well as inner stimuli was furthered by psychiatrist Allen Beck, who demonstrated that thoughts, peer influence and circumstance shape emotions. Beck's research formed the foundation of modern-day cognitive-behavioral therapy, the gold standard of emotional mastery as it's understood today.

The Role Of Emotional Mastery In Life And Society

Feelings and emotional mastery play a role in our subjective experience and interpersonal relationships.

- **Emotions unify us across cultural lines**. There are six basic emotions that are universal in all cultures: happiness, sadness, fear, anger, surprise and disgust. We all experience these feelings, although there are cultural differences regarding what's an appropriate display of emotion.

- **Emotions govern our sense of well-being**. Since emotions are a product of our experiences and how we perceive those experiences, we can cultivate positive emotions by focusing on them. There are 10 "power emotions" that cultivate emotional mastery by creating a base of positive affect. When we incorporate even small doses of gratitude, passion, love, hunger, curiosity, confidence, flexibility, cheerfulness, vitality and a sense of contribution, we set the stage for feeling good about ourselves.

- **Emotional mastery supports healthy relationships**. When you're able to demonstrate emotions that are appropriate to the situation, you're able to nurture your relationships. When you don't know how to master your emotions, the opposite occurs: You might fly off the handle at minor annoyances or react with anger when sadness is a more appropriate response. Your emotional response affects those around you, which shapes your relationships for better or worse.

Learning how to master your emotions is a skill anyone can build in six straightforward steps.

1. Identify what you're really feeling

The first step in learning how to master your emotions is identifying what your feelings are. To take that step toward emotional mastery, ask yourself:

- What am i really feeling right now?
- Am i really feeling…?
- Is it something else?

2. Acknowledge and appreciate your emotions, knowing they support you

Emotional mastery does not mean shutting down or denying your feelings. Instead, learning how to master your emotions means appreciating them as part of yourself.

- You never want to make your emotions wrong.
- The idea that anything you feel is "wrong" is a great way to destroy honest communication with yourself as well as with others.

3. Get curious about the message this emotion is offering you

Emotional mastery means approaching your feelings with a sense of curiosity. Your feelings will teach you a lot about yourself if you let them. Getting curious helps you:

- Interrupt your current emotional pattern.
- Solve the challenge.
- Prevent the same problem from occurring in the future.

4. Get confident

The quickest and most powerful route to emotional mastery over any feeling is to remember a time when you felt a similar emotion and handled it successfully. Since you managed the emotion in the past, surely you can handle it today.

5. Get certain you can handle this not only today, but in the future as well

To master your emotions, build confidence by rehearsing handling situations where this emotion might come up in the future. See, hear and feel yourself handling the situation. This is the equivalent of lifting emotional weights, so you'll build the "muscle" you need to handle your feelings successfully.

5. Get excited and take action

Now that you've learned how to master your emotions, it's time to get excited about the fact that you can:

- Easily handle this emotion.
- Take some action right away.
- Prove that you've handled it.

Learning emotional mastery is one of the most powerful steps you can take to create a life that's authentic and fulfilling.

Chapter 3:
7 Ways To Cultivate Emotions That Will Lead You To Greatness

Billions of men and women have walked the earth but only a handful have made their names engraved in history forever. These handful of people have achieved 'greatness' owing to their outstanding work, their passion and their character.

Now, greatness doesn't come overnight—greatness is not something you can just reach out and grab. Greatness is the result of how you have lived your entire life and what you have achieved in your lifetime. Against all your given circumstances, how impactful your life has been in this world, how much value you have given to the people around you, how much difference your presence has made in history counts towards how great you are. However, even though human greatness is subjective, people who are different and who have stood out from everyone else in a particular matter are perceived as great.

However, cultivating greatness in life asks for a 'great' deal of effort and all kinds of human effort are influenced by human emotions. So it's safe to say that greatness is, in fact, controlled by our emotions. Having said that, let's see what emotions are associated with greatness and how to cultivate them in real life:

1. Foster Gratitude

You cannot commence your journey towards greatness without being grateful first. That's right, being satisfied with what you already have in life and expressing due gratitude towards it will be your first step towards greatness. Being in a gratified emotional state at most times (if not all) will enhance your mental stability which will consequently help you perceive life in a different—or better point of view. This enhanced perception of life will remove your stresses and allow you to develop beyond the mediocrity of life and towards greatness.

2. Be As Curious As Child

Childhood is the time when a person starts to learn whatever that is around them. A child never stops questioning, a child never runs away from what they have to face. They just deal with things head on. Such kind of eagerness for life is something that most of us lose at the expense of time. As we grow up—as we know more, our interest keeps diminishing. We stop questioning anymore and accept what is. Eventually, we become entrapped into the ordinary. On the contrary, if we greet everything in life with bold eagerness, we expose ourselves to opportunities. And opportunities lead to greatness.

3. Ignite Your Passion

Passion has become a cliché term in any discussion related to achievements and life. Nevertheless, there is no way of denying the role of passion in driving your life force. Your ultimate zeal and fervor towards what you want in life is what distinguishes you to be great. Because admittedly, many people may want the same thing in life but how bad they want it—the intensity of wanting something is what drives people to stand out from the rest and win it over.

4. Become As Persistent As A Mountain

There are two types of great people on earth—1) Those who are born great and 2) Those who persistently work hard to become great. If you're reading this article, you probably belong to the later criteria. Being such, your determination is a key factor towards becoming great. Let nothing obstruct you—remain as firm as a mountain through all thick and thin. That kind of determination is what makes extraordinary out of the ordinary.

5. Develop Adaptability

As I have mentioned earlier, unless you are born great, your journey towards greatness will be an extremely demanding one. You will have to embrace great lengths beyond your comfort. In order to come out successful in such a journey, make sure that you become flexible to unexpected changes in your surroundings. Again, making yourself adaptable first in another journey in itself. You can't make yourself fit in adverse situations immediately. Adaptability or flexibility is cultivated prudently, with time, exposing yourself to adversities, little by little.

6. Confidence Is Key

Road to greatness often means that you have to tread a path that is discouraged by most. It's obvious—by definition, everybody cannot be great. People will most likely advise against you when you aspire something out of the ordinary. Some will even present logical explanations against you;especially your close ones. But nothing should waver your faith. You must remain boldly confident towards what you're pursuing. Only you can bring your greatness. Believe that.

7. Sense of Fulfilment Through Contributions

Honestly, there can be no greater feeling than what you'd feel after your presence has made a real impact on this world. If not, what else do we live for? Having contributed to the world and the people around you; this is the purpose of life. All the big and small contributions you make give meaning to your existence. It connects you to others, man and animal alike. It fulfills your purpose as a human being. We live for this sense of fulfillment and so, become a serial contributor. Create in yourself a greed for this feeling. At the end of the day, those who benefit from your contributions will revere you as great. No amount of success can be compared with this kind of greatness. So, never miss the opportunity of doing a good deed, no matter how minuscule or enormous.

In conclusion, these emotions don't come spontaneously. You have to create these emotions, cultivate them. And to cultivate these emotions, you must first understand yourself and your goals. With your eye on the prize, you have to create these emotions in you which will pave the path to your greatness. Gratitude, curiosity, passion, persistence, adaptability and fulfillment—each has its own weight and with all the emotions at play, nothing can stop you from becoming great in the truest form.

Chapter 4:
6 Concerning Effects of Mood On Your Life

By definition, mood is the predominant state of our mind which clouds over all the other emotions and judgements. Our mood represents the surface-level condition of our emotional self.

Mood is very versatile and sensitive. Subtle changes in our surroundings or even changes in our thoughts directly affect mood. And consequently, our mood, being the leader of our mental state, affects us, as a whole—even impacting our life directly.

Take notes of these following points so that you can overpower your mood and take complete control of your life.

Here Are 6 Ways How Changes In Your Mood Can Impact Your Life:

1. Mood On Your Judgement and Decision-Making

Humans are the most rational beings—fitted with the most advanced neural organ, the brain. Scientists say that our brain is capable of making one thousand trillion logical operations per second and yet still, we humans are never surprised to make the stupidest of judgements in real life.

Well, along with such an enormous 'Logical reasoning' capacity, our brains also come with an emotional center and that is where mood comes in to crash all logic. Most of the decisions we make are emotional, not logical. Since our emotions are steered by mood, it is no surprise that we often make irrational decisions out of emotional impulses.

But again, there are also some instances where mood-dictated decisions reap better outcomes compared to a logical decision. That's just life.

2. Mood Affects Your Mental Health

While our mood is a holistic reflection of our mental state caused by various external and internal factors, it is also a fact that our mood can be the outcome of some harboring mental illness. Both high degree of euphoria and depression can be an indication of mood disorder—just on two opposite ends of the spectrum.

There is no specific cause behind it except that it is a culmination of prolonged mood irregularities. And mood irregularities may come from anywhere i.e. worrying, quarrelling, drug abuse, period/puberty, hormonal changes etc. If such mood irregularity persists untreated, it may deteriorate your overall mental health and result in more serious conditions. So, consider monitoring your mood changes often.

3. Correlation Between Mood and Physical Well-Being

We have heard the proverb that goes, "A healthy body is a healthy mind". Basically, our body and mind function together. So, if your body is in a healthy state, your mind will reflect it by functioning properly as well. If on the other hand your body is not in a healthy state, due to lack of proper nutrition, sleep, and exercise, then your mind will become weak as well. Yes, according to research, having a persistent bad mood can lead to chronic stress which gradually creates hormonal imbalance in your body and thus, diseases like diabetes, hypertension, stroke etc. may arise in your body. Negative moods can also make you go age faster than usual. So having a cheerful mood not only keeps you happy but also fuels your body and keeps you young. Aim to keep your body in tip top condition to nourish the mind as well.

4. Effect Of Your Mood On Others

This is obvious, right? You wouldn't smile back at your significant other after you have lost your wallet, spilled hot coffee all over yourself and missed the only bus to your job interview.

Your mood overshadows how you behave with others. The only way to break out of this would be to meditate and achieve control over your emotional volatility—believe that whatever happened, happened for a reason. Your sully mood doesn't warrant being hostile with others. Instead, talk to people who want the best of you. Express your griefs.

5. Mood As A Catalyst In Your Productivity

Tech giants like Google, Apple, Microsoft all have certain 'play areas' for the employees to go and play different games. It is there to remove mental stress of the employees because mood is an essential factor in determining your productivity at work-place. According to experts, people with a negative mood are 10% less productive in their work than those who are in a positive mood. This correlation between mood and productivity is an important thing to be concerned about.

6. Mood Change Your Perspective

Everyone has their own point of view. Perspectives of people vary from individual to individual and similarly, it varies depending on the mood of an individual. On a bad day, even your favorite Starbucks drink would feel tasteless. It doesn't mean that they made a bad drink—it means that you're not in the mood of enjoying its taste. So, how you perceive things and people is greatly affected by your mindset. Pro-tip: Don't throw judgement over someone or something carrying a bad mood. You'll regret it later and think "I totally misread this".

Final Thoughts

Our mood has plenty of implications on our life. Though our mood is an external representation of our overall mental state, it has its effect on very miniscule aspects of our life to large and macroscopic levels. In the long run, our mood alone can be held responsible for what we have done our whole life—the choices we've made. Though it is really difficult to control our mood, we can always try. Meditating may be one of the possible ways to have our mood on the noose. Because no matter what happens, you wouldn't want your whole life to be an outcome of your emotional impulses would you?

Chapter 5:
5 Scientific Tricks To Become Perfectly Happy

Being happy comes naturally. Almost everything around us makes us happy in a certain way. Being happy is a constant feeling inside a human being. They always tend to get satisfied, even at a minimum. Everywhere we look nowadays, we see things filled with this bright emotion. We tune to the songs written about happiness, we see posters at every corner about being happy, and most importantly, we have people who make us happy. Being happy comes freely, without any fee.

There are scientific ways to become happy because an average human is always looking for more.

Some ways in which you'll feel full at heart and eased at mind. A burst of good laughter is like medicine to the core. So, science has given us ways to take this medicine without and cautions. Being happy is one of the least harmful emotions. It binds people together. Even some forms have been scientifically proven to work in favor of our happiness. There is almost no end to those bright smiles on our lips or those crinkles by our eyes. As it said, smiling is contagious. And we all prefer to smile back at everyone who smiles at us automatically. Here are some scientific ways to be happy.

1. **Minutes Into Exercise**

It is proven that some exercise helps you to smile and laugh more. If there is an exercise to be happy with, then people would be sure to give it a try now and then. Exercise helps us to regulate our jaw muscle, so it will be easier to pass a smile next time. There is also meditation. It enables you to calm your mind and leads towards an easier life. It usually helps to keep you at peace so you'll feel happier towards the things that should make you happy. You'll start to get more content at certain or small items. It becomes a habit slowly to smile more, be more satisfied. Being happy also benefits others, and then they will be more inclined to be pleased towards you.

2. **Get Enough Sleep**

Another scientifically proven way to get happy is to sleep enough every night. It helps with the formation of a proper mindset towards your happiness in life. Sleeping at least 8 hours a day is a must for being happy; if not, the 7 hours would suffice enough for you to smile a little more. It keeps your mind and soul at a steady pace, which is inclined to keep us calm and collected. Keeping calm and organized is one of the factors to be happy. Wake up early to listen to the birds or go for a morning run. Keep yourself fresh in the morning to be a better and happier person. Early to bed is a wise men choice. So, get a sound slumber every night to have a sunny morning following you.

3. Take A Break Now and Then

Even the greatest minds need some rest, so it's only average for a human to get some rest after a long period of working day and night. Go on a vacation. Get a leave because life needs to be enjoyed through anything. Working all the time makes you dull and unhappy. So, make sure to take a break once in a while to start again with a fresh mind and perform a better duty. Don't load yourself with the things that won't matter in a few years. Take vacation so you'll have a more peaceful time ahead of you in your life.

4. Build Your Happy Place

People tend to get tired quickly and often by working all the time. All most of the time, vacation can't seem like an option. So, the best place to visit in such a situation is your happy place—a place you have created in your mind where you are so glad all the time. Just by imagining such a place, you get comfortable and tend to keep working and being pleased with the same time. Your happy place gives you joy, and you become a happier person overall. And it is just easier to carry your vacation with you all the time.

5. Count Your Achievements

A great way to be scientifically happy is to count all the achievements you have made so far. Even count little things like watering plants as an achievement because it gives you a sense of joy. Achievements tell you that you have done more in your life than you intended to, and you will get motivated to do more every time. It makes you believe in yourself and get you going only forwards. You get happy with the deeds you have done till now, and it helps you plan your next good achievement. You naturally become more inclined to fulfill your desires and needs. All the things you have done so far will make you feel beneficial to society and happier for yourself.

Conclusion

Being happy is a great feeling with a more remarkable result in life. So, smiling more won't do you any wrong; in fact, it may be good for you to stretch your jaw a little. Happiness doesn't discriminate, so it will be good to spread this scientific happiness as much as we can. Being happy gives us a sense of undeniable joy and a vision of a positive and bright future.

Chapter 6:

7 EASY WAYS TO BE MINDFUL EVERY DAY

Mindfulness has a way of sounding complicated. It's anything but. "mindfulness is paying attention in a particular way: on purpose, in the present moment, non-judgmentally," there are many simple ways you can be more mindful. Here are seven tips to incorporate into your daily life.

1. Practice Mindfulness During Routine Activities

Try bringing awareness to the daily activities you usually do on autopilot. For instance, pay more attention as you're brushing your teeth, taking a shower, eating breakfast, or walking to work. Zero in on the sight, sound, smell, taste, and feel of these activities. "you might find the routine activity is more interesting than you thought,"

2. Practice Right When You Wake Up

"mindfulness practice first thing in the morning helps set the 'tone' of your nervous system for the rest of the day, increasing the likelihood of other mindful moments." If you find yourself dozing off, just practice after having your coffee or tea. But "...don't read the paper, turn on the tv, check your phone or email, etc. Until *after* you've had your 'sit,'"

3. Let Your Mind Wander

"your mind and brain are natural wanderers – much like a crawling toddler or a puppy. And that's a good thing. Having a "busy brain" is an asset. "the beneficial brain changes seen in the neuroscience research on mindfulness are thought to be promoted in large part by the act of noticing that your mind has wandered, and then non-judgmentally – lovingly [and] gently— bringing it back,"

4. Keep It Short

Our brains respond better to bursts of mindfulness. So being mindful several times a day is more helpful than a lengthy session or even a weekend retreat. While 20 minutes seems to be the gold standard, starting at a few minutes a day is ok, too. For instance, you can tune into your body, such as focusing "on how your shoes feel on your feet in that moment, or giving attention to how your jaw is doing [such as, is it] tight, loose or hanging open at the audacity of the person in front of you in the coffee line?"

5. Practice Mindfulness While You Wait

Waiting is a big source of frustration in our fast-paced lives – whether you're waiting in line or stuck in traffic. But while it might seem like a nuisance, waiting is an opportunity for mindfulness, halliwell said. When you're waiting, he suggested bringing your attention to your breath. Focus on "the flow of the breath in and out of your body, from moment to moment and allow everything else to just be, even if what's there is impatience or irritation."

6. Pick A Prompt To Remind You To Be Mindful

Choose a cue that you encounter regularly to shift your brain into mindful mode. For instance, you might pick a certain doorway or mirror or use drinking coffee or tea as a reminder.

7. Learn To Meditate

"the best way to cultivate mindfulness in everyday life is to formally train in meditation," practicing mindfulness is like learning a new language. "you can't just *decide* to be fluent in spanish – unless you already are – you have to learn the language first," "practicing meditation is how to learn the language of mindfulness." Meditation helps us tap into mindfulness with little effort. I suggest finding a local teacher or trying out cds.

Mindfulness isn't a luxury, "it's a practice that trains your brain to be more efficient and better integrated, with less distractibility and improved focus. It minimizes stress and even helps you become your best self." All of us have an emotional "set point." "some of us have more of a tendency toward withdrawal, avoidance, negative thinking and other depressive symptoms, [whereas] others have a greater tendency toward positive moods [such as, being] curious, tending to approach new things and positive thinking," through mindfulness, we may be able to train our brains and shift our set points. "mindfulness practice now has an abundance of neuroscience research to support that it helps our brains be more integrated, so your everyday activities, thoughts, attitudes [and] perceptions…are more balanced [or] well-rounded,"

Chapter 7:

7 Ways To Attract Happiness

We have seen a lot of people defining success as to their best of knowledge. While happiness is subjective from person to person, there's a law of attraction that remains constant for everyone in the world. It states that you will indirectly start to attract all the good things in life when you become happier. This is why happy people often have good lives where everything just somehow tends to work for them. Happiness not only feels good but can also make our manifestation attempts twice as effective. We shouldn't measure our happiness from external factors but instead, as cliche as it may sound, we should know that true happiness comes from the inside.

Here are some ways for you to attract happiness:

1. Make a choice to be happy:

When you choose to be as happy as you can in every moment of your life, your subconscious mind will start acknowledging your decision, and it will begin to find ways to bring more joy into your life. When you work towards your decision of being happy, the universe also plays its part and makes sure it attracts more situations in your life that you can be pleased about. The positive vibrations that you will give out will find their way back to you. You don't have to make the decision of being happy right away, as some of you might be going through a tough time. Sit, relax, and take some time to reflect on yourself first and then make a choice whenever you're ready.

2. Define What Happiness Means To You

We have also found ourselves asking this question a million times, "what exactly is happiness?" Some people would attach the idea of happiness with materialistic things such as a big house, expensive cars, branded clothes and shoes, designer bags, the latest technologies, and so forth. While for some, happiness is merely spending time with family and friends, doing the things that they love, and finding inner peace and calm.

3. React Positively under all situations:

We could experience a thousand good things but a million bad ones in our everyday lives. And sometimes, it could be complicated for us to encounter any kind of happiness given the circumstances. Although these circumstances cannot be in our control, how we react to them is always in our hands. As our favorite Professor Dumbledore once said, "Happiness can be found even in the darkest of times if only one remembers to turn on the light." Similarly, we should always try to find that silver lining at the end of the dark tunnel, always seek some positivity in every situation. But we are only humans. Don't try to enforce positivity on yourself if you don't feel like it. It's okay to address all our emotions equally till you be yourself again.

4. **Do not procrastinate:**

You might find it a bit weird, but procrastination does snatch your happiness away. No matter how much things are going well in your life, you would always find a loophole, a reason to be unhappy and dissatisfy with yourself a well as your life. Procrastination makes you believe that you are not living up to your fullest potential. You will get this nagging feeling that will eventually morph into negative emotions that would nearly eat you. So, try to avoid procrastination as much as possible and start doing the things that actually matter.

5. **Stay present:**

The key to becoming more focused, more at peace, more effective in manifesting, and eventually, much happier is to just live in the moment. Whatever you're doing in the present, try to be completely aware and focused on it. It will help you avoid all the negative feelings you have conjured up about the past and future. Try to stay present as much as you can; over time, it will become a habit, and you will develop the capability to face it all. This will definitely help you attract more happiness into your life.

6. **Do not compare yourself:**

As Theodore Rosevelt once said, "Comparison is the thief of joy." Whenever we compare ourselves to others, we tend to become ungrateful and strip ourselves of the ability to appreciate the good and abundance in our lives. We start to magnify the good in other people's lives and the bad that is in our own. We must understand that everyone is going through their own pace, and they all are secretly struggling with one thing or the other.

7. Don't try too hard:

Happiness demands patience. It is better to get into it gradually rather than being overeager. Many people take the law of attraction and being positive a little too far and start obsessing over it. They tend to panic if they get negative thoughts or are unable to attract the things they want. Don't get frustrated if things don't work out your way, and don't give up on the idea of happiness if you feel distressed. Try to prioritize your happiness and give others a reason to be happy too. Make yours as well as other's lives easy.

Conclusion:

Not many people know that, but being happy is actually the foundation towards attracting all your dreams and goals. When you adopt the habit of becoming truly happy every day, everything good will naturally follow you. Over time, happiness can even become your default state. Try your best to follow the guidelines above, and I guarantee that you will start feeling happier immediately.

Chapter 8:
6 Ways To Attract Your Potential

Do you sometimes feel like you're wasting your potential? And do you also feel unsure about how you can even reach your full potential? If so, you're like any other ambitious person who wants to make the best of his/her life. Because to me, that's what "reaching your potential" means.

We all have limited time on our hands. Some live longer than others. But you and I both know that it's not about how *long* you live, it's about *what you do* with the time you're alive. It's about leaving everything on the table and making sure you live up to your inner drive. Look, when I talk about reaching your potential, I'm not talking about what other people or society thinks we should do with our lives.

When you chase empty goals and objects, you become restless. Instead, chase your *own* potential and forget about everything external. Become the best person you can be. That's the only honourable aim there is. We identified 6 skills that will help you achieve your full potential. Here they are.

1. Self-Awareness

You must be comfortable with who you are and what you are. Don't try to be something you're not. And don't try to change yourself just because others tell you to. Instead, know who you are. And if you don't know, find out. Read, write, think, talk. That's self-awareness: It only requires you to be aware of your thoughts. And when you're self-aware, you automatically learn more about who you are—which is called self-knowledge. But it all starts with being aware. No awareness? No knowledge.

2. Leadership

First, focus on yourself. Fix your own problems. Become a stable person who you can rely on. When you do that, focus on inspiring others to do the same. The best way to help others is to teach them to rely on themselves. Sick and narcissistic people want to make people dependent on them. Leaders teach others to be independent. How? By setting a good example. There's no better way to lead.

3. Writing

Better writing leads to better thinking. And better thinking leads to better communication. Better communication leads to better results in your career. "What?! I never thought the writing was that important!" When you get good at one thing, it will help you to get better at other things. You see? It was only when I started writing that everything "clicked." When you become a better writer, you can easily express yourself and start making connections. That will improve your career in ways you never imagine.

4. Mindfulness

My definition of mindfulness might be different than yours. To be clear, I'm not talking about meditation, yoga, or Zen Buddhism. I'm talking about being a calm and mindful person. A person who's in control of their thoughts and emotions. A person who's solid as a rock. A person who others can rely on. But achieving that inner peace requires much training. I don't think we can ever fully master this skill. But by practicing control over our thoughts, we can get better. My favourite way to become more mindful is to be present. The more I *stay* in the present moment, the more mindful I am. The aim is never to be lost in thoughts. It's to be here.

5. Productivity

The funny thing about mindfulness is that people assume living in the present removes your drive to achieve your goals. The reverse is true. The more present I am, the more desire I feel to improve my life. And how do you improve your life? You already know it. I don't have to tell you that work is the only way to achieve things. Thinking about achieving your goals will not do anything real for you. Become a person who's productive *every day*. Make use of your time. Don't just waste it on watching tv, hanging out with your friends, gaming, or any other mindless routine activity. [Know how to get the most results in the least amount of time.](#) That's the ultimate aim of productivity skills.

6. Excellence

I half-assed many things in my life. "Let's just get it over with," was my motto. I was so impatient that I hardly did anything well. I just put in the minimum effort. Hence, I was never the best at anything. But then I realized that excellence is a skill. Look at Robert Greene who took 6 years to write another book. Or Lebron James who worked out during every off-season of his career. Or Helen Keller who published 5 books, despite being deaf and blind. But this is also true for successes that don't get attention in the media. Look at the top salesperson in any given organization who arrives early and leaves late every day. Or the mother who sacrifices nights out and dinner parties to raise her kid with all of her attention and love. That's called excellence.

Chapter 9:
7 Ways To Stop Overthinking And Relieve Stress

The way you respond to your thoughts can sometimes keep you in a cycle of <u>rumination</u>, or repetitive thinking. The next time you find yourself continuously running things over in your mind, take note of how it affects your mood. Do you feel irritated, nervous, or guilty? What's the primary emotion behind your thoughts? Having self-awareness is key to changing your mindset.

1. Find a distraction

Shut down overthinking by involving yourself in an activity you enjoy. This looks different for everyone, but ideas include:

- learning some new kitchen skills by tackling a new recipe
- going to your favorite workout class
- taking up a new hobby, such as painting
- volunteering with a local organization

2. Take a deep breath

You've heard it a million times, but that's because it works. The next time you find yourself tossing and turning over your thoughts, close your eyes and <u>breathe deeply</u>.

Try it

Here's a good starter exercise to help you unwind with your breath:

- Find a comfortable place to sit and relax your neck and shoulders.
- Place one hand over your heart and the other across your belly.
- Inhale and exhale through your nose, paying attention to how your chest and stomach move as you breathe.

Try doing this exercise three times a day for 5 minutes, or whenever you have racing thoughts.

3. Meditate

Developing a regular meditation practice is an <u>evidence-backed</u> way to help clear your mind of nervous chatter by turning your attention inward.

Look at the bigger picture

How will all the issues floating around in your mind affect you 5 or 10 years from now? Will anyone really care that you bought a fruit plate for the potluck instead of baking a pie from scratch?

Don't let minor issues turn into significant hurdles.

Do something nice for someone else

Trying to ease the load for someone else can help you put things in perspective. Think of ways you can be of service to someone going through a difficult time.

Does your friend who's in the middle of a divorce need a few hours of childcare? Can you pick up groceries for your neighbor who's been sick? Realizing you have the power to make someone's day better can keep negative thoughts from taking over. It also gives you something productive to focus on instead of your never-ending stream of thoughts.

4. Recognize automatic negative thinking

Automated negative thoughts (ANTs) refer to knee-jerk negative thoughts, usually involving fear or anger, you sometimes have in reaction to a situation.

Tackling ANTs

You can identify and work through your ANTs by keeping a record of your thoughts and actively working to change them:

Use a notebook to track the situation giving you anxiety, your mood, and the first thought that comes to you automatically.

As you dig into details, evaluate why the situation is causing these negative thoughts.

Break down the emotions you're experiencing and try to identify what you're telling yourself about the situation.

Find an alternative to your original thought. For example, instead of jumping straight to, "This is going to be an epic failure," try something along the lines of, "I'm genuinely trying my best.

5. Acknowledge your successes

When you're in the midst of overthinking, stop and take out your notebook or your favorite note-taking app on your phone. Jot down five things that have gone right over the past week and your role in them.

These don't need to be huge accomplishments. Maybe you stuck to your coffee budget this week or cleaned out your car. When you look at it on paper or on-screen, you might be surprised at how these little things add up.

If it feels helpful, refer back to this list when you find your thoughts spiralling.

6. Stay present

Not ready to commit to a meditation routine? There are plenty of other ways to ground yourself in the present moment.

Be here now

Here are a few ideas:

Unplug. Shut off your computer or phone for a designated amount of time each day, and spend that time on a single activity.

Eat mindfully. Treat yourself to one of your favorite meals. Try to find the joy in each bite, and really focus on how the food tastes, smells, and feels in your mouth.

Get outside. Take a walk outside, even if it's just a quick lap around the block. Take inventory of what you see along the way, noting any smells that waft by or sounds you hear.

7. Consider other viewpoints

Sometimes, quieting your thoughts requires stepping outside of your usual perspective. How you see the world is shaped by your life experiences, values, and assumptions. Imagining things from a different point of view can help you work through some of the noise

Chapter 10:
7 Reasons Why Comparison is The Thief of Joy

Comparison is a poison that creates feelings of jealousy and envy if we do not put reframe our pattern of thought. It is perfectly natural for us to engage in the habit of comparing our lives with those around us even if we had no business to do so.

When we scroll through social media, or hear stories of friends who have bought multi-million dollar properties, it's hard not to look at your own life and wonder what went wrong. Chasing other people's life even though they are not yours can only lead to nowhere.
Today we are going to find out 8 reasons why comparison is the ultimate thief of joy and happiness in our lives.

1. Feelings of Unworthiness

When we engage in comparisons with people who have fancy houses and cars, or those who have very successful careers, especially if they are friends of ours, it is hard not to feel sorry for ourselves. We feel inadequate and lacking. This inferiority complex only serves to remind us that we are lousy and useless, rather than the truth that we are special, unique, and amazing human beings who deserve to be respected and treated the same as people who are 1000x more successful than we are. No amount of success and wealth should make you feel unworthy in the presence of others.

2. We Feel Like We Are Not Where We Should Be

Comparing the amount of stuff and the level of career progression is not something that we should indulge in. That person we are comparing against may have some special talents, are gifted in areas of making money, or whatever reasons that landed them their position today, but that doesn't mean they are better than you. We are all on our own journeys - as long as we are on a path that we have set for ourselves, no matter how unglamorous it is, it is one that we should be proud of.

3. We Constantly Envy Others

Envy is not a good emotion to have, especially if it only makes us bitter at our life circumstances. We start blaming the things around us, our parents, our environment, and so on for the lack of success that we supposedly feel that we should have by now. There will always be someone richer and more successful than you, if you are never happy at where you are, you will never be really happy at all.

4. We Forget How Amazing Our Life Is

Engaging in comparisons is a sure fire way to help us forget how amazing our lives are. Suddenly everything you you own feels like trash next to someone who has something fancier. Your trusty Toyota feels like a garbage vehicle next to a Bentley, your nice condo suddenly feels like a mouse-hole next to that giant bungalow, and your well-to-do income suddenly seems like pocket money next a multi-million dollar earner. Always remind yourself that your life is amazing and that there are people in third world countries who are living life in poverty without proper food and shelter. You are living their dream life.

5. We Try To Force Our Way Into The Life That Others Are Living

By wanting what others have, you may have the tendency to copy their way of life. To try and emulate others, you are abandoning your own beliefs, goals, and dreams, to chase someone else's. You may attempt to climb that same mountain but you may never feel as happy as you are right now doing what you do for a lot less money and stress. People are all wired differently. Some may be workaholics who are able to spend 14 hours a day at the office while not caring about everything else in their life. Are you able to do the same? And are your priorities in life the same as well? If the answer is no, stick to your own path and be happy in it.

6. We Fail To Be Grateful For What We Have

It is perfectly easy to forget how grateful we should be to be alive. That we are born on this earth and we are gifted an opportunity to explore, create, and live. We fail to be grateful for the family and family in our lives, instead looking at the missing pool in our backyard or that extra zero in our bank accounts. Money can be earned and things can be bought, but family and friends only come once in your life. Don't forget you have all these things the next time you compare yourself with someone else.

7. We Are Never At Peace

We all want to have peace of mind. To be able to rest one day on our deathbed and say we have lived a great life. If even in our golden years, we are comparing ourselves with our peers who have achieved fancier things in life, we may only look back in life in regret rather than wonder. Don't waste your time comparing, instead celebrate and live each day in the present.

Conclusion

Focus on yourself. Focus on your journey. Focus on your own path to success. That is the only way forward that you should be striving for. You will be much happier for it. Be thankful that you are able to walk this earth and pursue your dreams. All will fall into place in time. I believe in you.

Chapter 11:
Seven Habits of Mentally Strong People

Mentally strong people also have great character and charming personalities because they can handle what ordinary people may not handle. Mental strength is the most desired trait by most people. To some, it is innate but others cultivate it over time through education or the school of life. Whichever way it is acquired, there are underlying habits that mentally strong people share.

Here are seven habits of mentally strong people:

1. <u>They Are Forgiving</u>

To err is human but forgiveness is divine. Forgiveness is difficult for most people to commit. It is seen as a sign of weakness but this is a fallacy. The contrary is true. Forgiveness is a measure of strength. When one person grossly transgresses another, the offended party will seek vengeance. He/she feels justified to revenge and until the offender 'pays' for his mistakes, the spirit of the offended will know no rest.

Mentally strong people are capable of forgiveness. This distinguishes them from the rest of the population. They understand that there is no point in re-visiting a matter when they can shelf it and prevent its repeat in the future. It does not mean that the offender has the license to continue hurting the other person. Instead, forgiveness sets the precedence that you are unaffected by the acts of an inconsiderate person. It demonstrates that your reasoning and emotions are not manipulated at will by someone who hurts you.

The next time someone wrongs you, let vengeance take the back seat and reason prevail over your actions. It is what mentally strong people do.

2. They Are Readers

There is nothing new under the sun. Everything that happens is a repetition of something that once occurred. To acquaint yourself with how history judged those who were once in your shoes, flip the pages of books and learn the signs of the time.

The habit of reading is not only for the literate. Even the illiterate can read, not books but the signs of the time and the harsh judgment of history on failures of men. Mentally strong people are wise not to learn from their mistakes but those of others. They unlearn the habits of failures and learn those of the successful.

Readership is a dynamic habit that is perfected by the mentally strong. They read the prevailing situations and adjust their actions accordingly. Reading builds the wealth of experience in life and prepares one on what action to take when confronted by a situation.

3. They Accept Criticism and Correction

Acceptance of correction from an authority displays humility. Correction and positive criticism are not to display your ignorance to the public but instead to inform you on a matter you were once ignorant about. Many people take criticism negatively and want to justify their actions. It is not always about being right or wrong – a concept that most people miss.

Embracing correction distinguishes mentally strong people from the faint-hearted who always rush to justify their acts.

The intelligence of the mentally strong is belittled when they engage in supremacy battles. They rise above the hate and become big brothers/sisters. Only a handful of a population can own up to their misinformation on a matter and humbly accept correction. Mentally strong people can display such levels of maturity.

4. <u>They Are Not Easily Discouraged</u>

It takes a lot to discourage mentally strong people. While ordinary people are stoppable in their tracks, it is not the same for the mentally strong. They are resilient to the adversity of whatever nature. They pursue their targets viciously and settle at nothing short of victory.

Mentally strong people may face a thousand ways to die but survive every one of them. They have the proverbial nine lives of the cat. Their determination is unmatched making them the envy of their peers who give up easily when challenged.

The majority of people in their curriculum vitae say that they can work under pressure. Unfortunately, their breaking point reaches sooner than expected. In the face of immense pressure at work, they yield to frivolous and unrealistic demands meted on them by busybodies. This is not the portion of the mentally strong.

5. <u>They Are Innovative</u>

Mentally strong people are not satisfied with the status quo. They always seek to unsettle the ordinary way of doing things. The traditional handling of affairs does not ogre well with them. There is always a new way of doing things.

Their mental strength is partly responsible for the adventurous spirit. The mentally endowed put their brains to work in solving human problems. They innovate simple life hacks, technology and come up with homemade solutions that were unknown before.

Innovation is not limited to the complicated science of experts. It also involves finding the simplest ways of solving problems in society. Innovation is habitual for mentally strong people.

6. They See The Bigger Picture

Life is a hunt for resources. Similar to the Lion, Mentally strong people do not lose focus of the antelope because of a dashing squirrel. To them, the point of reference is always the bigger picture. They interrogate every matter diligently to read between the lines because the devil always lies in the details.

It is not a matter of the emotions invoked in a discussion but the quality of reasoning devoid of any feelings. Mentally strong people can sieve needs from wants and decant fallacies from discussions.

7. They Are Bold

Fortune favors the bold. It is one thing to be decisive and another to boldly speak out your thoughts. Timidity is for mental infants (no offense). Mentally strong people are not afraid of giving their inputs in forums whenever required to because they speak from a point of knowledge.

Fearlessly talking about social ills and injustices is uncommon even among the political class. They lack the mental strength to engage fruitfully in matters of national importance. The bold is unafraid of how they may be challenged by other people because they are capable of seeing everybody's point of view. They appreciate the diversity in opinions.

The above are seven habits of mentally strong people. Mental strength wields untold power to those who possess it.

Chapter 12:
6 Ways To Define What Is Important In Your Life

In this crazy world that we live in, the course of evolution spirals upward and downward, and the collective humanity has witnessed glorious times and horrific ones. The events around us change minute-to-minute. So much seems out of our control, but we find solace in knowing that one thing remains within our immediate control; taking back ownership and responsibility for ourselves. If life has gotten away from you and you feel overwhelmed, anxious or depressed, then maybe it's time to stop and refocus on what's most important to you and find a way back to what really matters to you.

The idea is to evaluate what you're actually doing with and for yourself, determine if it's even essential to you, and then make the said necessary changes that will best accommodate your needs, interests, and desires. Here are some ways to consider how and on what things you should refocus your attention to determine what is most important in your life.

1. Determine What Things You Value Most

Choose and focus on the things around which you have to structure the life that you want to create. When you consciously make these choices, you are more focused on reminding yourself what things in your life you can't and won't do without. These all represent the backbone of your life. We often forget that people and events play a massive role in shaping up to our lives. They Mold us into what we have become so far and what we are to become in the future. Their support and encouragement in our lives are undeniable. We have to see which people and what events we value the most in our lives and then should keep our focus on them more.

2. Decide What Commitments Are Essential To You

Keeping the above valuable things in mind, evaluate which commitments do you value the most in your life. Commitments are the obligations you enter into willingly and represent your promise to see any relationship/project/contract conclusion steadfastly. Renegotiate your essential commitments, if necessary, but consider completing the existing commitments that you are already obligated to and refuse to take any new ones if you aren't ready. That way, you will focus more and fulfill those commitments first that are more significant to you and your life.

3. Assess The Way You Use Your Time

Most of us have a fixed daily routine, with many fixed activities, habits, and chores. Evaluate which things are absolutely necessary and vital for shaping up your life and yourself daily. Assess the time you spend communicating, how much of your time you spend online, emailing, texting, or on your cell phone. How can you cut back the amount of time spent on these activities to do something more productive? How much time are you spending on TV, radio, reading newspapers and magazines? Consider decreasing your consumption and receive the basic information from a reputable source only once throughout the day. Avoid repetition and redundancy.

4. Get Rid of Any clutter That's In Your Life

Look around you and see, do you need everything you have? Give away anything that you haven't used since the last two years. It could be anything, from selling items to furniture, clothing, shoes, etc. Anything that you no longer need. Someone else can happily use what you haven't all this time. And not just the worldly things; get rid of all the emotional and psychological clutter you have kept aside for so long, and it no longer serves you. We have to get rid of the old things to make room for the new things to come. This will help us reflect on our actual being of who we are and where we are.

5. Spend More Time With People That Matter To You

Evaluate how much quality time you actually spend with your family and close friends. As life evolves, more people will enter into your sphere. These people may fall into different categories of importance in your life, such as acquaintances, colleagues, friends, partners, etc. Our time is precious, so it is wise to use it on those that matter to us the most. It's necessary to sort out our interactions and to assess the meaning of each relationship to us.

6. Make Time To Be Alone

It all comes down to how much time do you make yourself at the end of the day? What was the last time you spent doing something you're passionate about or what you love doing? Give yourself all the time and permission to express your creativity and make peace with your mind. Take care of your body, spirit, and mind because these are the things that will make you feel alive. Take a walk and look around, reacquaint yourself with all the beauty around you. Make each breath count.

Conclusion

Identifying and understanding your values is a challenging but as well as an essential exercise. Your personal values are a central part of defining who you are and who you want to be. By becoming more aware of these significant factors in your life, you can use them as your best guide in any situation. It's comforting and helpful to rely on your values since most of our life's decisions are based on them.

Chapter 13:
7 Ways To Know When It's Time To Say Goodbye To The Past

Holding on to someone or something and fearing to let go is a problem that many of us will struggle with at some point or another. Be it a partner, career, or item, a history has been built around that and we find it hard to move on and leave this treasured piece behind.

Whether it be a 6months or 10 years, it can be hard for us to come to terms with letting go because we have invested so much time, energy, and soul, into it. Governed by emotions, we hold on to them even though it may no longer bring us happiness or joy.

Whatever the reasons are, here are 7 ways that can help you say goodbye to the past and invite better things into your life:

1. You've Drag things For Way Too Long

If it's a career that you're holding on to, you may feel that you've invested a lot of effort and energy in it, waiting for the time that you will get promoted. But the days come and go, months turn into years, and you find yourself a decade later wondering what happened. Letting things drag on is no way to live life. Time is precious and every moment we waste is a moment we can never get back.

2. You Know It's Time

People may tell us we're happy and that we should be so lucky to have this job or that person in our lives, but no one can hide the unhappiness that is festering within us. Deep down in our hearts, we understand ourselves more than any other people ever would. And we know, subconsciously, if it's time to move on and let go of the past. If you are unsure, do some soul-searching. Find a time to sit by yourself quietly, or go for a retreat on your own. Sort out your feelings and bring some clarity to yourself.

3. It No Longer Brings You Joy

With a person who we have spent so much energy being a relationship with over the years, it can be hard to come to terms with the reality that he or she no longer makes you feel happy or loved anymore. Being in a constant state of unhappiness is no way to live our lives. We have every power in us to make decisions that serves us rather than hinder us. Acknowledge and accept these feelings of unhappiness. Use it as fuel to make that important decision that you know you must make.

4. You Are Holding On Out of Fear

Many a times we hold out on ending that relationship with something because we live in a constant state of fear. Career-wise we may resign ourself to the fate that things are just the way it is and we are afraid that we may never find another job again. So we hold on to that false sense of security and just drag your feet till retirement. Relationship wise, we hold on to them because we fear we may never find someone else again. So we let fear keep us in these places, feeling more and more trapped in the process.

5. You're Afraid of the Unknown

It is human nature to be afraid of the unknown. If we cannot see a clear path ahead, most of us would not dare to travel down that road. We don't know if the grass will be greener on the other side if we quit our jobs, and we don't know what the dating world will be like after being out of it for so long. We lose confidence in believing the unknown is a magical place and that wonderful things can happen there if we let ourselves take the leap of faith. That was how we got to where we were in the first place before we realized it no longer served us anymore.

6. You're Ready For Change

This is similar to the second point about knowing it's time with one key difference - you know that you ready for a new phase of life. Having the urge to intact change in your life, you believe that you don't want to be stuck in whatever situation you are in anymore. You desperately want to make things better. Embrace these feelings and start taking strong action to force change to happen for you.

7. You Know You Deserve Happiness

Happiness has to be earned. Happiness doesn't just happen to you. If you know you deserve to be happy, and that the current thing you are holding on to only brings you sorrow, it is time to let it go. Only when you let go of what's holding you down can you make room for better and brighter things. Putting yourself out there in the face of trials and errors is the only way you can find what you are truly looking for. Demand happiness and expect it to happen to you.

Conclusion

Saying goodbye to the past is not easy, and not everyone has the courage or strength to do it. You can either choose to live in fear, or you can choose to live a brave life. It is time to make that critical decision for yourself at this crossroad right now. Only one choice can bring you the life that you truly desire. So choose wisely.

Chapter 14:

Five Habits For A Beautiful Life

A beautiful life means different things to different people. However, there are some things that we can all agree about. It is a happy one. Some of us have chased this kind of life but it has proven elusive to the brink of throwing in the towel. We play a greater role in designing a beautiful life for ourselves than others do in our lives.

Here are five habits for a beautiful life:

1. Live The Moment

This is not a call to carelessness. The focal point is to cherish the present moment. We are often distracted by our past experiences even in times when we ought to celebrate our current wins. The present is beautiful because we can influence it.

A beautiful life is joyous and the envy of those who cannot experience it. Savor the present completely and do not be entangled in the past. The past will withhold you from leveraging the opportunities popping up presently. Every saint has a past and every sinner has a future. You can shape the future by living in the moment and not dwelling in the past.

Worrying about the future is not beneficial. If you can change a situation, why worry? If you cannot also change anything, why worry? It is pointless to take the burden of occurrences that are yet to happen. Enjoy your present successes while you can and lead the beautiful life you have been dreaming of.

2. Plan Wisely

Like everything invaluable, a beautiful life should be planned for. Planning is an integral part of determining whether a beautiful flawless life is achievable or not. It is not an event but a process that requires meticulous attention.

Planning entails extensive allocation of resources to life priorities. You should get your priorities right for things to run smoothly. In planning, your judgment and conscience should be as clear as a cloudless night. Any conflict of interest that could arise will jeopardize the attainment of a beautiful life - the ultimate goal.

We may be forced to make some painful sacrifices along the way and possibly give up short-time pleasures for long-term comfort. It may bring some discomfort but is worth the attainment of a beautiful life. Planning is a heavy price that must be made a routine to anyone aspiring to this magnificent dream.

3. Pursue Your Purpose

Your purpose is the sole reason that keeps you going in life. You should pursue what motivates you to keep chasing your dreams. A beautiful life is one of fulfillment. Your purpose will bring it effortlessly if you remain loyal to it.

Focusing on your purpose can be a daunting task to an undisciplined mind. Many distractions may come up to make you stray or shift goalposts. You need to be disciplined to continue treading in the narrow path of your purpose. Do not lose sight of the antelope (a beautiful life) because of a dashing squirrel (distractions).

Living a life of purpose will satisfy you because you will willfully do what brings you joy; not what circumstances have forced you to. A cheerful way to live each day like it is your last is by finding pleasure in your routine activities and by extension, your purpose. Pursue it boldly!

4. Cut Your Coat According To Your Cloth

Live within your means and cut on unnecessary costs. Many people struggle to live within a particular social class that they are not able to afford at the moment. In the process of fitting in, they incur unmanageable debt.

A beautiful life does not mean one of luxury. It is stress-free and affordable within your space. It is unimaginable that one will wear himself/herself out to live a lifestyle beyond reach. Societal pressure should not push you to the brink of self-destruction as you try to fit in other people's shoes.

Even as you work towards your goals, do not suffocate yourself to please other people. Accept your financial status and make your budget within it. You will have an authentic and beautiful life.

5. Share Your Life With Your Loved Ones

We all have our families and loved ones. Our parents, siblings, spouses, and children should share our lives with us. It is beautiful and desirable that we intertwin our social and personal lives. The warmth and love of our families will put a smile on our faces despite any challenges.

Often, our families are the backbone of our emotional support. We retreat to them when we are wounded by the struggles of life and they nurse us back to health. Their presence and contribution to our lives are immeasurable. Family does not necessarily mean you have to be related by blood.

Some people are strong pillars in our lives and have seen us through hard times. Over time, they have become part of our family. We should share our lives with them and treasure each moment. We would be building a beautiful life for ourselves and the upcoming generations.

These are five habits we need to develop for a beautiful life. We only live once and should enjoy our lifetime by all means.

Chapter 15:
6 Ways To Achieve Peak Performance

To be successful requires much more than just your intelligence and talent. There are basic needs which have to be met to function at your peak. These basic needs are neglected by most, impairing their capacity to rise to those elusive higher levels of success and happiness in life.

1. Get enough sleep

Sleep deprivation means peak performance deprivation. Without proper sleep you wake up to meet the day feeling scatterbrained, foggy and unfocused. You grab your cup of coffee to get a charge on your brain, which completely depletes your brain function over the course of the day, making your brain even more exhausted.

Good sleep improves your ability to be patient, retain information, think clearly, make good decisions and be present and alert in all your daily interactions. Sleep is your time off from problem solving.

When you get the proper rest your brain becomes awake, alive and ready to generate the cognitive prowess and emotional regulation you need to function at your peak performance.

2. Drink lemon water

Lemon water is a great substitute for your morning coffee. Although lemons do not contain caffeine, lemon water has excellent pick-me-up properties without negative side effects. It energizes the brain, especially if it is warm, and hydrates your lymph system.

Among the most important benefits of lemon water are its strong antibacterial, antiviral, and immune-boosting power, making sick days from work nearly non-existent. Lemon water cures headache, freshens breath, cleanses the skin, improves digestion, eliminates PMS with its diuretic properties and reduces the acidity in the body.

Most importantly, lemon water increases your cognitive capacity and improves mood with its stimulating properties on the brain, helping you to operate more consistently in your peak performance zone.

3. Get daily exercise

Exercise is the best way to reduce the stress that impairs your performance stamina. Exercise increases your "happy" mood chemicals through the release of endorphins. Endorphins help rid your mind and body of tension alleviating anxiety helping you to calm down.

The brain needs physical activity to stay flexible. Exercise stimulates neurogenesis, or the growth of new brain cells, which improves overall brain function. The development of new brain cells keeps your brain young and in shape, allowing you to be more efficient, pliable and clear in your decision making, higher thinking and learning capacities. Neurogenesis is the catalyst to peak performance.

Further, there is nothing that can bring down self-esteem quicker than not liking how you look. Exercise improves self-confidence and your perception of your attractiveness and self-worth. This confidence contributes greatly to your success, prompting people to respect you and take you seriously.

4. Have emotional support

Having healthy, loving relationships increases your happiness, success and longevity by promoting your capacity to function in life as your best self. Social connectedness and love gives you relationships to be motivated for and people to be inspired by.

A strong social network decreases stress, provides you with a sense of belonging and gives your life the deeper meaning it needs. When you are loved and loving, and carving out quality time to cultivate these relationships, you are exalted, elevated and encouraged to live your dreams fully.

5. Be unapologetically optimistic

A requirement of peak performance is to look for the best in every situation. Optimism is the commitment to believe, expect and trust that things in life are rigged in your favor. Even when something bad happens, you find the silver lining.

A positive outlook on life strengthens your immune system and the emotional quality of your life experiences, allowing you to be resilient in the face of fear, stress and challenge.

Being an optimist or a pessimist boils down to the way you talk to yourself. When you are optimistic you are fierce in the belief it is your own actions which result in positive things happening. You live by positive affirmation, take responsibility for your own happiness and anticipate more good things will happen for you in the future.

When bad things happen you do not blame yourself, you are simply willing to change yourself.

6. Have time alone

Time alone is refueling to your physical, mental, emotional and spiritual self. This time recharges you, helping to cultivate your peak performance levels again and again. You must give yourself time to recover from the stress of consistently being around others. Being around people continuously wears down your ability to regulate your emotional state, causing self-regulation fatigue. For this reason you must give yourself permission to take the pressure off and disconnect.

Chapter 16:
7 Signs You're More Attractive Than You Think

We feel conscious about ourselves every now and then. We are our own biggest critics. Finding flaws in ourselves sometimes leads to constructive criticism, which in turn leads to self-development. But sometimes, the constructive criticism might lead to a self-destructive reproach that will disturb the healthy and happy life you're living. It's normal to have self-doubts, wondering how people see us or what they think about us.

We live in a society where there is constant pressure to look your best self. People might point out our flaws and weaknesses, but what matters is how we emerge from it all. A study by Feynman in 2007 revealed that the way people see us determines how they will treat us. So, it's best if we remain confident and comfortable in our skin. Our appearances can either make or break the first impression of how people will perceive us. Research in 2016 by Lammers, Davis, Davidson, and Hogue revealed that first impressions could have a lasting effect on our relationship with the other person.

Many of us are used to being hard on ourselves. So it practically seems like a joke that anyone would find us attractive. Here are 7 signs that will confirm that you're more attractive than you think!

1. You rarely get compliments:

I know many of you wouldn't believe this but just hear me out first. Have you ever put on your most fabulous outfit, put on that sexy cologne, and dressed up all stunning from head to toe? You were confident enough that all eyes would be on you, and you will receive tons of compliments. But by the end of it all, you have hardly received any! Naturally, this would lead to you having some severe self-doubts about yourself. But you needn't worry. Psychology says that whenever we see a gorgeous person, we assume that he/she might have very high self-esteem. As a result, people rarely compliment those people. People also think that you already know how stunning you look, and you might be getting a lot of attention already. So, they avoid complimenting you too much. Instead of treating the scarcity of compliments as a bad thing, just maybe you are already the subject of many secret admirers.

2. The Compliments you get feel insincere:

Finally, you're receiving those compliments that you have been waiting for, for so long. But to your surprise, they sound apathetic and emotionless. You're confirmed now that you don't come off quite as attractive to other people. But we have a theory on this too. Suppose there is a gorgeous friend of yours. Do you constantly flatter them and gush about their appearance? You don't. You only compliment them if they're wearing a new outfit or changed their looks. The same happens to you. People think you already know how beautiful you are, so they don't pay much attention to the compliments they give you. The sole reason why the compliments sound so mundane and trivial. So, if you have been experiencing this, then you're more attractive than you think.

3. **People get nervous around you:**

Whenever you enter a room, you notice people suddenly being all nervous around you. This may happen because they're caught off guard by how gorgeous you look. They may feel pressured to make an excellent first impression since you've already made a perfect one on them. As a result, they try to hide their flaws in In front of you. They might become either too confident or underconfident. People tend to become awkward and nervous when they see other people as too attractive or too perfect.

4. **You find yourself locking eyes with a lot of people:**

We, humans, tend to stare at the desirable things we want. Research by the University of Oslo in 2015 found that your brain gives you a dopamine shot when you look at something pleasurable. While it may not always be the case that people staring at you might find you attractive. Sometimes it can just be a mistake, or maybe you have worn your shirt wrong, or there's something stuck on your teeth, but a lot of times, we stare and lock eyes with the people we find good-looking. So, if a person keeps staring at you even if you have caught them and passes a smile, it definitely means he likes what he's staring at.

5. People are surprised by your insecurities:

People might become shocked when you tell them about your complexes and insecurities. They think that since you're so gorgeous, you have nothing to worry about. But we all have our bad days where we go through self-doubts and low self-esteem. People wouldn't see this as such a problem because they would love to look like you and don't even notice the flaws you point out about yourself. Instead, they might become irritated when you complain about your issues because you look so self-confident and self-sufficient to them.

6. People are often too polite or too unfriendly to you:

You find people being either too optimistic or too pessimistic around you. They either might be too warm and friendly or too harsh and rude when you first meet them. The truth is, people, tend to react strongly to the people they find attractive. Some people might find excuses to spend time with you and praise you, while others may sound too petty around you. This might also be because of the jealousy they may feel towards you. A positive person will always see you as an equal and will always treat you with a polite and friendly attitude.

7. People are interested in you:

You might feel people asking a lot of questions about you and getting to know you better. They carry the conversation and like talking to you from time to time. Even though your communication skills are pretty average, they would still speak to you with the same interest. This is because they might think that you would have a great personality. After all, you have a pretty face. They would become compromising and would jump at the first opportunity to help you. We tend to be friendlier and more generous to the people subconsciously we find attractive. By helping you, they want to look good in your eyes too.

Conclusion:

You need to look past your insecurities, embrace your flaws, and accept the characteristics that people value in you. Don't forget that in the end, a good heart always wins over good looks. Don't become a victim of societal pressure and mould yourself into a perfect and flawless human being. There is nothing more attractive than appreciating yourself with all the good and the bad and knowing your worth. Find happiness in being vulnerable and weak, through the tough and challenging times. Life is a roller coaster ride, so you shouldn't have a need to feel perfect all the time!

Chapter 17:
<u>6 Ways To Deal With Betrayal</u>

Betrayal is a strong word. And the most challenging part of it is recovery. Healing from something someone has done to you that you were not in favor of can be as hard as counting the number of hair on your head. The first thing that comes in our way is our emotions. Anger, rage, and regret. But, what can one do to save themselves from such a move? They can only be careful with the people around them. Trust issues have always been challenging to deal with. And betrayal only fuels that fire. We often turn to others for support, and sometimes they turn out to be deceivers. It may leave us unprotected.

No doubt that betrayal changes someone to some extinct. The person may feel insecurities within themselves. They start to doubt and stress themselves. It often leads to self-harm, too, at times. And the most severe of them all would be anxiety. Because no matter what, we can't ignore the fact that someone has lied to us and made us believe them. Betrayal is painful. And it's common to have experienced it once in your life. When someone you trusted with your secrets or emotions has broken that trust, that feeling of not being valued enough makes us hate that person, whether they did it intentionally or unintentionally. But there can be some ways to deal with betrayal.

1. Take Time For Emotional Improvement

After a heartbreak, what we need is time. Time to think, time to process, and time to heal. We can't instantly forget about anything that has happened to us. "Time heals all wounds." And that is precisely what we should do. Take a break. Try to do things you want. Make yourself feel light and collected. Stay away from the person who hurt you. This way, it will help you bury that memory quickly. Try to think about it as little as possible. Make sure you have other things on your mind instead. Rearrange your priorities from the start. This time you believe in yourself more than you felt in that person.

2. Overcome Self-Hatred

It is often that you would feel hatred towards yourself. Because you sometimes believe that it was your fault, to begin with. The thing with betrayal is that it is one-sided. The other person can do nothing but suffer. Naturally, you would be pitying yourself for their actions and feeling insecure. But it's not worth your time or emotion. You need to get a hold of yourself and talk some sense into yourself.

3. Try To Forgive and Forget

We all know that it is not as easy as it sounds, but it is more beneficial. When someone betrays us, we feel the need to take revenge. Hurt them the way they hurt us. But nothing can be as comforting as forgetting it ever happened. We all will remember a part of it, but it doesn't have to come between your life. It takes a lot of determination to forgive someone you don't want to ignore, but you will see the pros of it in the future. If you decide you take revenge, then it will leave you guilty and regretful in the future.

4. Ask For Help From The Trusted

It may be difficult for you to trust anyone after being betrayed. But you can always go to someone for comfort. If a possible third party can support you, don't hesitate to reach out to them. Make sure you talk about it with someone so you can take advice and feel light. It will help you to deal with the situation quickly. It will give you the peace of mind that will help you all along the journey ahead. It is recommended to talk with someone who had a betrayal in their life.

5. Acknowledge, Don't React

There is a significant difference between responding and reacting. We should be in control of our emotions. We need to acknowledge our feelings. After betrayal, our senses are more likely to be mixed up, leaving us confused. But that is a recipe for disaster. It will only be harmful to you to react without analyzing the situation appropriately. You can't ignore the fact that you have been hurt, but you will feel calmer by the time.

6. Be Careful Next Time

No one can ensure that we won't get hurt again. But we can be careful around people. That doesn't necessarily mean having trust issues with people but detecting the people who can hurt you. And with each time, you will get better and better at dealing with betrayal. It would help if you felt those emotions to overcome them every single time. And after each series of betrayals, you will become stronger than before.

Conclusion

Betrayal can be heart-wrenching, but it should not stop you from being happy in life. Cry and grieve for a day or two. And then get up again as a stronger person. Believe in yourself. Let go of the past and focus on your future, for it can bring much more happiness.

Chapter 18:
6 Ways To Get People To Like You

We are always trying for people to like us. We work on ourselves so that we can impress them. Everyone can not enjoy a single person. There will always be someone who dislikes them. But, that one person does not stop us from being charming and making people like us. In today's generation, good people are difficult to find. We all have our definition of being liked. We all have our type of person to select. That makes it very hard for someone to like someone by just knowing their name. We always judge people quickly, even to understand their nature. That makes it hard to like someone.

People always work their selves to be liked by the majority of people. It gives you a sense of comfort knowing that people are happy with you. You feel at ease when you know that people around you tend to smile by thinking about you. For that, you need to make an excellent first impression on people. Training yourself in such a way that you become everyone's favorite can sure be tiring. But, it always comes with a plus point.

1. **Don't Judge**

If you want people to like you, then you need to stop judging them. It is not good to consider someone based on rumors or by listening to one side of the story. Don't judge at all. We can never have an idea of what's going on in an individual life. We can not know what they are going through without them telling us. The best we can do is not judge them. Give them time to open up. Let them speak with you without the fear of being judged. Assuming someone is the worst without you them knowing is a horrendous thing to do.

2. **Let Go of Your Ego and Arrogance**

Make people feel like they can talk to you anytime they want. Arrogance will lead you nowhere. You will only be left alone in the end. So, make friends. Don't be picky about people. Try to get to know everyone with their own stories and theories. Make them feel comfortable around you to willingly come to talk to you and feel at ease after a few words with you. Being egotistic may make people fear you, but it will not make people like you. Be friendly with everyone around you.

3. **Show Your Interest In People**

When people talk about their lives, let them. Be interested in their lives, so it will make them feel unique around you. Make sure you listen attentively to their rant and remember as much as possible about a person. Even if they talk about something boring, try to make an effort towards them. If they talk about something worth knowledge, appreciate them. Ask them questions about it, or share your part of information with them, if you have any on that subject. Just try to make an effort, and people will like you instantly.

4. **Try To Make New Friends**

People admire others when they can click with anyone they meet. Making new friends can be a challenge, but it gives you confidence and, of course, new friends. Try to provide an excellent first impression and show them your best traits. Try to be yourself as much as possible, but do not go deep into friendship instantly. Give them time to adapt to your presence. You will notice that they will come to you themselves. That is because they like being around you. They trust you with their time, and you should valve it.

5. **Be Positive**

Everyone loves people. You give a bright, positive vibe. They tend to go to them, talk to them and listen to them. People who provide positive energy are easy to communicate with, and we can almost instantly become friends. Those are the type of people we can trust and enjoy being around. Positivity plays a critical role in your want to be liked. It may not be easy, but practice makes perfect. You have to give it your all and make everyone happy.

6. **Be Physically and Mentally Present For The People Who Need You**

People sometimes need support from their most trusted companion. You have to make sure you are there for them whenever they need you. Be there for them physically, and you can comfort someone without even speaking with them. Just hug them or just try to be there for them. It will make them feel peaceful by your presence. Or be there emotionally if they are ready. Try to talk to them. Listen to whatever they have to say, even if it doesn't make sense. And if they need comfort. Try to motivate them with your words.

Conclusion

You need to improve yourself immensely if you want people to like you. Make sure you do the right thing at the right time. Make people trust you and make them believe your words. Even a small gesture can make people like you. Have the courage to change yourself so that people will like you with all their heart's content.

Chapter 19:
3 Steps To Choose Mind Over Mood

Have you ever said something out of anger that you later regretted? Do you let fear talk you out of taking the risks that could really benefit you? If so, you're not alone.

Emotions are powerful. Your mood determines how you interact with people, how much money you spend, how you deal with challenges, and how you spend your time.

Gaining control over your emotions will help you become mentally stronger. Fortunately, anyone can become better at choosing their mind over their mood. Just like any other skill, managing your emotions requires practice and dedication. Managing your emotions isn't the same as suppressing them. Ignoring your sadness or pretending you don't feel pain won't make those emotions go away.

In fact, unaddressed emotional wounds are likely to get worse over time. And there's a good chance suppressing your feelings will cause you to turn to unhealthy coping skills--like food or alcohol. It's important to acknowledge your feelings while also recognizing that your emotions don't have to control you. If you wake up on the wrong side of the bed, you can take control of your mood and turn your day around. If you are angry, you can choose to calm yourself down.

Here are three ways to gain better control over your mood:

1. Label Your Emotions

Before you can change how you feel, you need to acknowledge what you're experiencing right now. Are you nervous? Do you feel disappointed? Are you sad?

Keep in mind that anger sometimes masks emotions that feel vulnerable--like shame or embarrassment. So pay close attention to what's really going on inside of you.

Put a name your emotions. Keep in mind you might feel a whole bunch of emotions at once--like anxious, frustrated, and impatient.

Labeling how you feel can take a lot of the sting out of the emotion. It can also help you take careful note of how those feelings are likely to affect your decisions.

2. Reframe Your Thoughts

Your emotions affect the way you perceive events. If you're feeling anxious and you get an email from the boss that says she wants to see you right away, you might assume you're going to get fired. If however, you're feeling happy when you get that same email, your first thought might be that you're going to be promoted or congratulated on a job well done.

Consider the emotional filter you're looking at the world through. Then, reframe your thoughts to develop a more realistic view.

If you catch yourself thinking, "This networking event is going to be a complete waste of time. No one is going to talk to me and I'm going to look like an idiot," remind yourself, "It's up to me to get something out of the event. I'll introduce myself to new people and show interest in learning about them."

Sometimes, the easiest way to gain a different perspective is to take a step back and ask yourself, "What would I say to a friend who had this problem?" Answering that question will take some of the emotion out of the equation so you can think more rationally.

If you find yourself dwelling on negative things, you may need to change the channel in your brain. A quick physical activity, like going for a walk or cleaning off your desk, can help you stop ruminating.

3. Engage in a Mood Booster

When you're in a bad mood, you're likely to engage in activities that keep you in that state of mind. Isolating yourself, mindlessly scrolling through your phone, or complaining to people around you are just a few of the typical "go-to bad mood behaviors" you might indulge in.

But, those things will keep you stuck. You have to take positive action if you want to feel better.

Think of the things you do when you feel happy. Do those things when you're in a bad mood and you'll start to feel better.

Here are a few examples of mood boosters:

- Call a friend to talk about something pleasant (not to continue complaining).
- Go for a walk.
- Meditate for a few minutes.
- Listen to uplifting music.

Keep Practicing Your Emotional Regulation Skills

Managing your emotions is tough at times. And there will likely be a specific emotion--like anger--that sometimes gets the best of you.

But the more time and attention you spend on regulating your emotions, the mentally stronger you'll become. You'll gain confidence in your ability to handle discomfort while also knowing that you can make healthy choices that shift your mood.

Chapter 20:

6 Signs You Need To Give Yourself Some Personal Space

While we wish to stay forever in the honeymoon phase of a relationship, we also must keep in mind that it is precisely what we call it; only a phase. Not every relationship is sunshine and rainbows every day. A relationship is between two individuals who both have individual needs. Sometimes, those needs include having some alone time with themselves. But how and when exactly do you know if you need some space from your partner?

April Masini, a New York-based relationship expert and author, says, "If you can't make it an hour or two without checking in or asking a question of your partner, you need a break." Needing space in your relationship does not in any way means that you don't love your partner anymore; it simply means that you need some time to get recharge and take care of yourself. Here are some signs that you need to give yourself some personal space.

1. You Feel Stressed Out

Suppose you're unnecessarily stressed out, even if it isn't coming from your relationship. In that case, it's probably a good idea to spend some alone time and ponder over things. It can be some underlying tension coming from work or family, or it might be something in your relationship that you want but are not necessarily getting it. Taking some time out for yourself and figuring out where your stress is coming from or what's been upsetting you, you will then be better positioned to sort out your problems and discuss those issues with your partner.

2. You Don't Feel Like yourself

A significant sign indicating that you need some alone time for yourself is if you are started to feel exhausted, irritable, or simply just not yourself. Everyone should know the importance of needing some me time for yourselves. Your partner should understand if you need to take care of yourself and your mental health. Needing space from your partner in no way means that your relationship is at stake or if there's anything wrong with it. It simply means that you both need to spend time with yourself to rest, relax, or spend time with other people.

3. You Feel Suffocated

Spending so much time with people can prove fatal and can lead to being co-dependent on them, which is ultimately the kiss of death. It is assumed that, as a couple, you both should naturally be spending all of your time together, but there is such a thing as seeing too much of each other. It is essential to pull away and have some time for yourself. Find a hobby, take a walk, read a book. The more you spend your time with a person, the more likely you will get tired of each other soon. You need to get yourself some personal space not to get suffocated and overwhelmed by your relationships with other people.

4. You Don't Have any Outside Interests

Do you have any interests of your own, or do you rely entirely on the other person and their hobbies? It's healthy to have some things in common with your partner, but not all of them. Suppose you follow and copy their hobbies and interests and don't have any of your own. In that case, it might lead to some adverse psychological effects. Suppose they leave you or are just too busy to see you; you'll be left with nothing but boredom and waiting for the other person to catch up to you again. You need to give yourself space and find out what you like as an individual. Find your hobbies and passions, grow fond of them, and then work on them independently.

5. Spending Time With Them Is Draining You Out

If you aren't having as much fun as you used to have while meeting them, then you should take some space for yourself. If you're feeling drained out and low on energy after every interaction, it's time to spend some time apart. You get frustrated and irritated easily and don't make any efforts to resolve a fight. Patch-ups seem challenging for you; if your interactions are painful and difficult, then consider some alone time to gather your thoughts.

6. Your Vibe's Getting A Bit Off

Although there can be many reasons for this, stress, depression, exhaustion, etc., the primary cause can be that you're not getting enough space to deal with your emotions and feelings. Your relationship feels strained, and you feel like escaping from everything. This is the best time to ask for space from everyone and everything and ponder over whatever's bothering you.

Conclusion

Everyone deserves a relationship with more positivity than negativity in it. It's okay to need some space for yourself now and then. Evaluate your needs and try to figure out what you want.

Chapter 21:
7 Ways To Live Together In Harmony With Your Partner

A harmonious relationship can make a person's life happy and beautiful, but, unfortunately, not all of us are blessed with a harmonious relationship. It is essential to work on your relationship in order to make it work. Creating a harmonious bond between you and your partner can make your relationship more healthy and stable. The dream relationship of everybody is to feel loved, accepted, and respected but to achieve such a relationship, and you need to first work on yourself. You need to make sure that you are doing your best at making your partner feel loved.

Most people nowadays want to find their soulmates, but even when they see their soulmates, they don't have a peaceful relationship; the lack of harmony causes this.

Here are 7 ways to live together in harmony with your partner.

1. Accept Your Partners The Way They Are

The first step to a harmonious relationship is acceptance. It would be best to accept your partners the way they are; distancing them from yourself because of a simple mistake can lead to a toxic relationship. If you choose to love a person and be with them, you need to accept the good and bad in them. As they say that no one is perfect, we all are a work in progress. When you cannot receive your partner the way they are, a harmonious relationship cannot be achieved. It would help if you allowed them to evolve and support them throughout this journey.

2. Be Gentle And Compassionate

When you embody gentleness and compassion, your relationship bond deepens, and there is harmony in the relationship. Instead of jumping to conclusions and reacting dramatically, you need to respond with gentleness and understand your partner's feelings.

Compassion brings grace to a person. To achieve a harmonious relationship, you should give your partner grace to work on themselves, understand, and give them space to evolve and mature. It may take time, but it strengthens a relationship.

3. Expectations Should Be Released

With expectations comes disappointment. Expectations are the unspoken standards you expected your partner to live up to. When your partner does not live up to your expectations, you might feel upset or disappointed, but how can you have such high expectations from your partner about things that are unspoken. Work on letting go of these ideals that the society and your subconscious mind created about how a relationship should be. Release the attachment to situations turning out a specific way. Brace yourself for different outcomes of different situations. Don't expect too much from your partner because your partner, like you, cannot always live up to your expectation.

4. Personal Space In A Relationship

Every human being needs personal space; we often see couples that are always together. It may feel exciting and comforting at first, but everyone needs their personal space to think and function properly. After being with each other with no personal space, one can start feeling suffocated and may behave negatively. It would help if you had time to breathe, to expand, and to look within. To evolve, you need space. Personal space between couples proves that their relationship is healthy and robust.

5. Honesty

Honest communication is not just a factor to achieve a harmonious relationship but also to have any relationship at all. Not being truthful can cause conflicts and problems in a relationship. Moreover, being a liar can be a toxic trait that can cause your partner to end the relationship. But before being honest with your partner, you need to be honest with yourself. Know your true self, explore the good and bad in yourself. Don't hide your mistakes from your partner; instead, be honest and apologize to them before it is too late. Honesty is a crucial factor in achieving a harmonious relationship.

6. Shun Your Ego

Ego and harmony cannot simply go hand in hand; where ego exists, harmony cannot be established. Often by some people, ego is considered a toxic trait. This is the ego that stops a person from apologizing for his mistakes, which can create tension among the couple. The stubbornness to do things your way is caused by ego and can easily result in unwanted scenarios. These are not the components of a healthy relationship. So to establish a harmonious relationship, you should remove ego and learn to compromise a bit. By removing ego, you allow yourself to be more flexible and understanding.

7. Let Go if Unnecessary Emotional Pain

When you keep hurting over old resentments, you convert that pain into toxic feelings that are not good for a relationship. These poisonous feelings can make you make some bad decisions that may result in your partner feeling unsafe around you. This pain can cause you to bury your positives feeling inside. As a result of this, you may feel pessimistic and may exaggerate minor conflicts into something more. A person must let go of this emotional stress and pain. You can let go by going to a therapist or yoga and meditation. Once you have let go of the pain, your heart is now open to a peaceful and harmonious relationship.

To establish a harmonious relationship, you have to accept and understand your partner and work on yourself. Also, work on your radical integrity.

Chapter 22:

6 Reasons Your Emotions Are Getting In The Way Of Your Success

Do you ever ponder on why your new year's resolutions fail miserably? It is primarily because of the toxic emotions and our negative thoughts of the past that keeps us stuck with the same patterns and regrets. We can try to change and manage our attitudes well, but the emotions are out of our hands. So even though we can't control what we feel, we must confront them to achieve our goals and resolutions.

A therapist in Tarzana, California, Vicki Botnick, explains that any emotion – even elation, joy, or others you would typically view as positive – can intensify to a point where it becomes difficult to control.

Here are 6 Reasons why emotions are getting in the way of your success

1. You let your emotions rule you

Most of us are clueless about taking control of our emotions and how they affect our productivity. But we must manage them if we strive to achieve our goals. Emotions are an instant response to a specific trigger. All of our emotions are interlinked with each other. For example, we can't taste the satisfaction of joy if we don't go through any pain, or we can't enjoy courage without being fearful first. All of these emotions are what make us human. Embracing both negative and positive emotions are essential, but if they start to get in the way of your success, then you must take action and act upon them.

2. Anger.

"The greatest remedy for anger is a delay." - Thomas Paine.

Anger is the majorly common emotion that humankind feels. This negative emotion can result from frustrations, conflicts, mistreatment, or interpersonal conflicts, or is sometimes triggered by an event or experience that happened in the past. For example, suppose you studied really hard for a test but didn't get the expected grade. The next time when you're willing to give it another try, you won't study as much as you did the first time because you'll remember your previous failed attempt. You will re-live your failure and will eventually become frustrated and demotivated. The best thing to do in this scenario is just to take some time off and breathe. Distance yourself from everything and get yourself to calm down before making any decision. Ask yourself then, are you too hard on yourself? Are you trying to do everything at once that's causing you to get upset? Have you set the bar too high? Ponder on these questions and then look for the solutions calmly. Being angry about the things you can't control is pointless, as anger feeds more anger, and you would get stuck in an endless loop of resentment and frustration. Seek solutions on the things you can control and be patient.

3. Fear.

The fear of failure is perhaps the worst emotion we can endure. It snatches away even the slightest chance of taking that first step to achieving our dreams and goals. The reasons why we are so afraid of failures may vary from person to person. Some people can't digest that they are full of flaws and that failure is the most crucial step towards leading a successful life. They want to win no matter what. Others might feel that they are not good enough if they can't achieve something. Most people don't admit that they have fears. Fear can either be your greatest friend or your worst enemy; it all depends on how you treat it, whether you look into its eyes and face it or run from it. Living fearlessly doesn't mean that a person isn't afraid of anything, but rather that the person has befriended his fears and is now dancing with them. One shouldn't run away from the challenges that the world throws at him, but stand up to them bravely and face them. Make a list of all the things that scare you or are distracting you from achieving your goals. And then work towards them until they no longer bother you or gets in the way of your success. A famous African proverb states, "Smooth seas do not make skillful sailors."

4. Envy.

Bertrand Russell once said, "Beggars do not envy millionaires, though of course, they will envy other beggars who are more successful." Envy and jealousy are the two strongest emotions that mankind has experienced. Although they go hand in hand with each other, there is still a slight difference between them. Being envious wants the other person's things, while jealousy wants the other person's recognition from others. Whenever things tend to go south, we start to become envious of those who are successful. We compare ourselves to them, idealize their successes, and in the process, we lose ourselves. We shift our focus from our signs of progress to being demotivated and stressed out. Pain is an indicator of progress. When we stretch our minds beyond our comfort zone, we feel pain. This pain is the indication that we should move forward and not run away. We shouldn't compare our initial progress to those who have been striving for years. Everyone has their own pace. We should focus on ourselves and setting our potentials free.

5. **Guilt.**

The guilt of doing something else or saying something else instead of what you already did or said will forever haunt us. Guilt gets us stuck in the past rather than live in the present moment. There is a term in psychology, The Zeigarnik Effect, which refers that people remember uncompleted tasks more than the completed ones. They then blame themselves for not doing it sooner or better. Our mindset is often linked with productivity blame, where we feel bad for achieving something or not working hard enough. We tend to punish ourselves emotionally and get the idea that we can never reach our goals. But it is essential to take some time off and treat yourself with kindness and empathy. Don't over-pressurize yourself. Self-appreciate and become a better version of yourself in the process. "Mistakes are always forgivable if one dares to admit them." - Bruce Lee.

6. **Sadness.**

"We must understand that sadness is an ocean, and sometimes we drown, while other days, we are forced to swim." - R.M. Drake.

Feeling sad or low on energy crushes productivity and enthusiasm. We feel demotivated and can't focus on our tasks. Sadness makes us feel secluded and isolated. We must embrace this emotion at our own pace, but we shouldn't hide away from whatever it is that's bothering us. Start again slowly with your productivity, make slight progress, start rechallenging yourself. But don't do all of this unless you feel okay again.

Conclusion:

Understanding how your emotions are getting in the way of your productivity requires practice. Self-awareness is the key to know yourself better, so you can deal with your emotions efficiently. Please pay close attention to what your feelings are trying to tell you rather than running away from them.

Chapter 23:

6 Relationship Goals To Have

We live in a generation where the term "relationship goals" has become a part of the trendy vernacular. It may seem more like a hashtag than anything else, but we all are eager to go into the depth of its meaning. A beautiful photo of a stunning couple having a good time together? Relationship goals. A cute text message sent to a girlfriend from his boyfriend? Relationship goals. A perfect wedding? Relationship goals. All these might seem sweet and enviable and look like an absolute dream, and it doesn't mean that these come off as accessible to them. If you have ever been in a relationship, you would know exactly what I'm saying.

Love is not always fireworks, passion, and butterflies. Relationships are not just date nights, kisses, and cuddles. And love is not that glamorous as it looks on social media. But when you strive to build something together, involving your selflessness, commitment, and even sweat and tears, those are actual relationship goals. Here is a list of what relationship goals you must have with your partner.

1. **Always Do New Things Together**

Sure, alone time might be great, but together time is where the magic happens too. Avoiding your relationship becoming mundane and a rut, you both should try to do new things together. This could be choosing any vacation spot or having an exciting adventure together. You both should make a list of all the things you want to do with each other and keep adding stuff that might pop later. Tick things off as you go, and you'll never run out of things to do together.

2. Be Each Other's Biggest Supporters

Perhaps one of the best things about being in a relationship is that you'll always have someone in your corner. Regardless of how crazy or unrealistic your dreams and goals may sound, your partner should be your biggest supporter. Seeing the person you love believing in could come off as a massive motivation to achieve your goals. This goes both ways; both men and women need to feel emotionally supported. You both should take some time out to discuss what emotional support looks like to you, what and when you need it, and then provide the said support for each other.

3. Put Each Other First

Putting each other first in your relationship will ensure that you're paying attention to each other's needs and making sure they are being met. You have become selfless with each other, and you both strive to make each other happy and would do anything to put a smile on each other's faces.

You complement each other, protect each other, support and love each other, no matter the obstacles or circumstances.

4. Know The Importance of Alone Time

As much as you don't want to keep your hands off your partner in the early stages of your relationship, it's essential to know that you both need time alone to recharge and refill your cup. Spending all of your time together isn't sustainable, and alone time is significant. It will help you maintain your individuality, allow you breathing space, and encourage a closer relationship with each other when you spend time together.

5. Keep The Physical Connection Going

Sex isn't always an option when dealing with different phases of your relationship. There are going to be times when it might not be physically or mentally possible. But this in no way means that you should stop all physical connections. Physically touching the person you love releases an oxytocin hormone; this feel-good love hormone reduces stress and makes you feel wonderful things. You can stay physically connected by holding hands, cuddling, or simply leaning on one another.

6. Speak Positively About Each Other

Speaking ill of your partner with others is not only disrespectful to them, but it's also disrespectful to your relationship. Sure, you can vent in tough times, but make sure you talk about the actions and behaviors that upset you and not their personality traits. Always speak positively and kindly of each other. Even if their behavior irritates you, focus more on the characteristics you love of them and let it pass.

Conclusion

Relationships are complicated but beautiful at the same time. As simple as the above factors may sound to you, these things take a lot of effort and hard work to be implemented. But when you do all of these with the person you love the most in the world, then all of it can be worth it.

Chapter 24:
6 Signs You Are Emotionally Unavailable

In times of need, all we want is emotional comfort. The people around us mainly provide it. But the question is, will we support them if the need arises? You might be emotionally unavailable for them when they need you. It is necessary to have some emotional stability to form some strong bonds. If you are emotionally unapproachable, you will have fewer friends than someone you stand mentally tall. It is not harmful to be emotionally unavailable, but you need to change that in the long run. And for that, you need to reflect on yourself first.

It would help if you always were your top priority. While knowing why you are emotionally unapproachable, you need to focus on yourself calmly. Giving respect and talking is not enough for someone to rely on you. You need to support them whenever needed. Talk your mind with them. Be honest with them. But not in a rude way, in a comforting way. So, next time they will come to you for emotional support and comfort. If you are relating to all these things, then here are some signs that confirm it.

1. You Keep People At A Distance

It is usual for an emotionally unavailable person to be seen alone at times. They tend to stay aloof at times; that way, they don't have to be emotionally available. And even if you meet people, you always find it challenging to make a bond with them. You might have a few friends and family members close to you. But you always find meeting new people an emotionally draining activity. You also might like to hang out with people, but opening up is not your forte. If you are emotionally unavailable, then you keep people at a hands distance from you.

2. You Have Insecurities

If you struggle to love yourself, then count it as a sign of emotional stress. People are likely to be unavailable emotionally for others when they are emotionally unavailable for themselves too. We always doubt the people who love us. How can they when I, myself, can't? And this self-hatred eventually results in a distant relationship with your fellow beings. Pampering yourself time by time is essential for every single one of us. It teaches us how one should be taken care of and how to support each other.

3. You Have A Terrible Past Experience

This could be one of the reasons for your unapproachable nature towards people. When you keep some terrible memory or trauma stored inside of you, it's most likely you cannot comfort some other being. It won't seem like something you would do. Because you keep this emotional difference, you become distant and are forced to live with those memories, making things worse. It would help if you talked things out. Either your parents or your friends. Tell them whatever is on your mind, and you will feel light at heart. Nothing can change the past once it's gone, but we can work on the future.

4. You Got Heartbroken

In most cases, people are not born with this nature to be emotionally unavailable. It often comes with heartbreak. If you had a breakup with your partner, that could affect your emotional life significantly. And if it was a long-term relationship, then you got emotionally deprived. But on the plus side, you got single again. Ready to choose from scratch. Instead, you look towards all the negative points of this breakup. Who knows, maybe you'll find someone better.

5. You Are An Introvert

Do you hate going to parties or gatherings? Does meeting with friends sound tiresome? If yes, then surprise, you are an introvert. Social life can be a mess sometimes. Sometimes we prefer a book to a person. That trait of ours makes us emotionally unavailable for others. It is not a bad thing to stay at home on a Friday night, but going out once in a while may be healthy for you. And the easiest way to do that is to make an extrovert friend. Then you won't need to make an effort. Everything will go smoothly.

6. You Hate Asking For Help

Do you feel so independent that you hate asking for help from others? Sometimes when we get support from others, we feel like they did a favor for us. So, instead of asking for help, we prefer to do everything alone, by ourselves. Asking for aid, from superior or inferior, is no big deal. Everyone needs help sometimes.

Conclusion

Being emotionally unavailable doesn't make you a wrong person, but being there for others gives us self-comfort too. It's not all bad to interact with others; instead, it's pretty fun if you try. It will make your life much easier, and you will have a lot of support too.

Chapter 25:
3 Ways To Master Your Next Move

"I don't know what to do with my life!" If you find yourself saying this, you're not alone. It's common for people to get to a point where they feel stuck or directionless. It can result from poor decision making or an inability to make decisions at all.

This state of not knowing what to do next applies to a lot of people, at any age and at different times in your life.

Personally, I have discovered that following these 5 steps will help you to find out what to do with your life, feel good, and get unstuck.

1. Get Moving and Clear Your Mind

"Not knowing what you want is a lot better than knowing exactly what you want but not being able to get it, at least you have hope."

I once faced a very challenging and emotional time; all I could do was think about what I needed to do to get to the next day.

There were no thoughts of what I wanted to do in the future nor were there any thoughts of how I wanted my life to be. It was just a matter of surviving from one day to the next.

For me, during this challenging time, when I was telling myself, "I don't know what to do with my life," exercise was the solution to helping me get through my day.

Every morning my alarm would go off at 6 am. I would have my running gear ready by the bed. I would get dressed, walk out the door, and start running for 45 minutes.

For a long time, it was hard to get out of bed and go for my run because I just wanted to hide away. Over time, I began to look forward to my morning run as I felt more energized, and I was sleeping better.

2. Wake Your Conscious Mind and Limit Choices

"Nobody is going to do your life for you. You have to do it yourself, whether you're rich or poor, out of money or making it, the beneficiary of ridiculous fortune or terrible injustice…Self pity is a dead end road. You can make the choice to drive down it. It's up to you to decide to stay parked there or to turn around and drive out." -Cheryl Stryed.

Life isn't predictable, and the solutions we seek to answer our life questions don't always come nicely wrapped. There are no rules to follow, and you have to work hard to define your life pathway when you don't know what to do with your life.

Waking our conscious minds to accept our reality and embrace change is one step toward finding out what we need to do next in our life.

We become paralyzed rather than liberated by the power of choice. When we are presented with too many options, our brain doesn't know what to do with it all.

Research has shown that there is a sweet spot when it comes to choices. If we have too few, we feel limited. If we have too many, we feel overwhelmed.

How does this translate to your everyday life? If you're changing career fields and aren't sure what to switch over to, limit your options to five or six possible areas. Choose to mark one off the list every few days once you've sat with the choices a bit. As your brain focuses on fewer and fewer choices, it will become easier to see the direction you genuinely want to go in.

3. Take Small Steps With a 30-Day Challenge

In order to reprogram your conscious mind and stop saying "I don't know what to do with my life," set yourself a 30-day challenge.

You may ask, why 30 days? Because this is how the small steps you take gradually become your powerful habits

Setting a deadline has a powerful effect on motivation. Research has shown time and again that deadlines, even those that are self-imposed, can reduce procrastination and lead to better decision making.

Try setting one to three goals to be achieved during your 30-day challenge. Maybe you want to learn to code. Set weekly goals related to free online courses, and by the end of the month you'll have a good deal of knowledge under your belt.

Or perhaps you want to spend more time with your kids. Make a goal to have one family night each week where you offer all of your attention to your kids. You can even let them help plan what you will do on that special night.

Achieving these goals after one month will give you the confidence and self belief to keep going. It also helps you avoid doing nothing while you're feeling stuck. Once you know you can achieve one goal, you'll go on to achieve more and more.

Chapter 26:
6 Signs You Have A Fear of Intimacy

Intimacy avoidance or avoidance anxiety, also sometimes referred to as the fear of intimacy, is characterized as the fear of sharing a close emotional or physical relationship with someone. People who experience it do not consciously want to avoid intimacy; they even long for closeness, but they frequently push others away and may even sabotage relationships for many reasons.

The fear of intimacy is separate from the fear of vulnerability, though both of them can be closely intertwined. A person who has a fear of intimacy may be comfortable becoming vulnerable and showing their true self to their trusted friends and relatives. This problem often begins when a person finds relationships becoming too close or intimate. Fear of intimacy can stem from several causes. Overcoming this fear and anxiety can take time, but you can work on it if you know the signs of why you have the fear in the first place.

1. **Fear Of Commitment**

A person who has a fear of intimacy can interact well with others initially. It's when the relationship and its value grow closer that everything starts to fall apart. Instead of connecting with your partner on an intimate level, you find ways and excuses to end the relationship and replace it with yet another superficial relationship. Some might even call you a 'serial dater,' as you tend to lose interest after a few dates and abruptly end the relationship. The pattern of emerging short-term relationships and having a 'commitment phobia' can signify that you fear intimacy.

2. Perfectionism

The idea of erfectionism often works to push others away rather than draw them near. The underlying fear of intimacy often lies in a person who thinks he does not deserve to be loved and supported. The constant need for someone to prove themselves to be perfect and lovable can cause people to drift apart from them. Absolute perfectionism lies in being imperfect. We should be able to accept the flaws of others and should expect them to do the same for us. There's no beauty in trying to be perfect when we know we cannot achieve it.

3. Difficulty Expressing Needs

A person who has a fear of intimacy may have significant difficulty in expressing needs and wishes. This may stem from feeling undeserving of another's support. You need to understand that people cannot simply 'mind read,' they cannot know your needs by just looking at you; this might cause you to think that your needs go unfulfilled and your feelings of unworthiness are confirmed. This can lead to a vicious cycle of you not being vocal about your needs and lacking trust in your partner, and your relationship is meant to doom sooner or later.

4. Sabotaging Relationships

People who have a fear of intimacy may sabotage their relationship in many ways. You might get insecure, act suspicious, and accuse your partner of something that hasn't actually occurred. It can also take the form of nitpicking and being very critical of a partner. Your trust in your partner would lack day by day, and you would find yourself drifting apart from them.

5. Difficulties with Physical Contact

Fear of intimacy can lead to extremes when it comes to physical contact. It would swing between having a constant need for physical contact or avoiding it entirely. You might be inattentive to your partner's needs and solely concentrate on your own need for sexual release or gratification. People with a fear of intimacy may also recoil from sex altogether. Both ends of the spectrum lead to an inability to let go or communicate intimately emotionally. Letting yourself be emotionally naked and bringing up your fears and insecurities to your partner may help you overcome this problem.

6. You're Angry - A Lot

One way that the deep, subconscious fear of intimacy can manifest is via anger. Constant explosions of anger might indicate immaturity, and immature people are not able to form intimate relationships. Everyone gets angry sometimes, and it's an emotion that we cannot ignore, even if we want to. But if you find that your feelings of anger bubble up constantly or inappropriately, a fear of intimacy may be lurking underneath. Don't deny these intimacy issues, but instead put them on the table and communicate effectively with the person you are interested in.

Conclusion

Actions that root out in fear of intimacy only perpetuate the concern. With effort, especially a good therapist, many people have overcome this fear and developed the understanding and tools needed to create a long-term intimate relationship.

Chapter 27:
5 Habits For An Extremely Productive Day

Our productivity and efficiency during the day are variables of several factors. Some days seem better, the sun a little brighter than normal; the food tastes sweeter and the mood lighter. In such days, unmatched joy bubbles within us increasing our productivity exponentially. Many people cannot choose when to experience these days. Instead, they are at the mercy of their emotions and the influence of other people who can ruin their day whenever they please.

Here are five habits for an extremely productive day:

1. <u>Plan For Your Day Beforehand.</u>

Failure to plan is planning to fail. A plan is an integral part of success. It means that you understand the obligation you have to live the day ahead and the duties and responsibilities in your in-tray. A plan will help you check all the boxes on your to-do list and you can track your progress in each.

In planning for your day, you will know the resources that you have and those that you lack. It is also possible to budget on your means earlier rather than waiting for the actual day and start scampering for resources. A wise man does not live on a borrowed budget but within his own.

A good plan is a job half done. Your day will be more productive when nothing takes you by surprise because you would have anticipated every occurrence beforehand and it will find you armed with a solution.

2. <u>Wake Up Early</u>

The early bird catches the worm. Punctuality is very important if you want to have a productive day. An early riser has a fresh and clear mind compared to those who wake up late and start their routine fast because they are behind schedule. They do not have the advantage of calmness and composure because they want to make up for time lost. This exposes them to error and ridicule from their enemies if they fail, which is imminent because of their inaccuracy.

When one wakes up early, one has an advantage over other people. They can open their businesses or start their work earlier than their competitors do. They maximize their productivity because they have created enough time for each task they had scheduled. Consider waking up early to have an extremely productive day.

3. <u>Do Not Bite More Than You Can Chew</u>

This calls for sobriety in the handling of tasks and designing of goals. The pressure to outdo yourself can be overwhelming enough to make you lose focus on what is at stake. It is paramount to set realistic and achievable goals so that you can concentrate on them. Shun anything that presents itself to you that is beyond your ability no matter how attractive it seems.

The power of self-control is at play. Resist the temptation of going out of your way to prove a point for the sake of it. Instead, fully concentrate on what you had planned. Schedule anything outside your plan to the following day. It is far from procrastination because in this case, you have a clearly defined timeline on when to actualize your plans.

Failure to develop this habit will lead you to a situation where you have many unfinished tasks. This is not productivity, by all standards. Focus on what you can manage and do it efficiently.

4. <u>Avoid Negative Company</u>

A negative company will derail your progress and work. When you associate yourself with such people, you will not see the unseen benefit in challenges and instead, you will focus on the undone, incomplete, and failed bits of your work. Failure is contagious. If you constantly surround yourself with a clique of failures, you too shall fail.

To have a productive day, have friends who share your vision. You will blossom under their shade and they will encourage you in your work. This will show you possibility even when you see failure and doom. In their company, your days will be productive and joyful.

5. <u>Look At The Bigger Picture</u>

As you seek to have productive days, look at the bigger picture. It will make you focus on the greater plan you have rather than petty squabbles and meaningless distractions that come your way. The bigger picture will always remind you of your cause and inspire you to live up to it even when challenges come your way.

When you pay attention to the above five habits, you will have extremely productive days. It all lies in your effort to adopt them.

Chapter 28:
7 Signs Of An Incompatible Relationship

You might have heard the word 'compatibility' a million times before starting a new relationship or even after getting into one. But what exactly does the word 'compatibility' means? Compatibility is when you and your partner not only share the same interests but also share the same values, goals, have compatible libidos, support each other in their times of distress and frustration, help them achieve their dreams, make each other feel safe, and plan a future where you can both see each other being together and happy. However, not every couple is blessed with the joys of having a compatible relationship. Melody Kiersz, a professional matchmaker, says, "There are some obvious ones, like not wanting the same things in life, lifestyle choices in terms of travel or location, and relationship style (I.e., monogamous vs. Polyamorous)."

No matter how much in love you are with your partner and how desperately you compromise in your relationship to make everything seem better, if you both aren't compatible, then the relationship might have a dead-end in the long run. Here are some signs that will help you see if you are in an incompatible relationship.

1. **Your partner doesn't respect the differences:**

There's rarely a time when you might feel that you have found a person just like you. People are different from each other. Sometimes, their passion or goals may align with yours, but some differences are always there. You may like to read a book or watch a movie in your free time instead of your partner playing a video game or going outdoor with their friends. If your partner doesn't respect the differences and forces you to change your hobbies and dreams, then it's a red flag. After all, respect is the critical element to any lasting relationship. In an incompatible relationship, your partner might make you feel bad about being different from them and may mock you about the different things you do.

2. **Your partner gets overly jealous:**

We, as human beings, cannot wholly eliminate the factor of jealousy from within ourselves. Being jealous and possessive of your partner isn't a bad thing, as long as you have it under control. But if your partner gets overly jealous of petty things, keeps a regular check on you and your whereabouts, and constantly bugs you, then it will not only make you frustrated, but you will eventually be exhausted, and your mental health will shamble. This isn't just a sign of incompatibility but also a sign of toxicity.

3. **You're a different version of yourself around them:**

What is a relationship if you don't even feel comfortable around your partner? Out of all the people, your love interest should be the one with whom you can be yourself and not pretend. You find yourself always pretending to be a perfect flawless creature because they might have said something or showed you that they wouldn't accept the things that your real version does. The constant struggle of making yourself look ideal in Infront of your partner's eyes would eventually drain you out. You might stop pretending after a while, and your partner may or may not like it. If your partner doesn't like the real you, then you should consider this as an incompatible relationship and move on.

4. Lack of communication:

A lasting relationship is based on communicating effectively with your partner. For example, suppose you feel like your partner discards your feelings and consider them stupid after you tell them that something's been bothering you or tells them that something they've said might have hurt you. In that case, your partner is being emotionally unavailable and doesn't value your feelings. As a result, you might feel uneasy about opening up to them, and they might feel the same about you. This is one of the significant reasons for the incompatibility between the partners. If you aren't ready to share your feelings with them or get ignored if you share them, the relationship will eventually come down the hill.

5. Your partner does not take care of your wants and needs:

Consider this, and you have just come home after a long day of work, hoping to get some rest. As soon as you arrive, there is a long pile of dishes waiting for you, and your partner tells you to make something for dinner. Yep, you can imagine the reaction your partner would get. A relationship should be based on mutual efforts and understanding. If your partner is doing the bare minimum and you find yourself putting in all the efforts, then you definitely don't deserve to be with a person like them. Instead, your partner should treat you special every now and then, makes you realize your worth in his life, takes care of you, and make small gestures to show his love.

6. Fighting gets ugly with them:

Arguing and fighting are the forte of every relationship. What matters is how you resolve the issue after you've argued or fought. In a compatible relationship, couples always try to sort out the things bothering them, and they eventually apologize to each other. While in an incompatible relationship, you would find your partner constantly bickering and mocking long after the fight has ended. You both won't see eye to eye with each other for days and may go to bed angry at each other. Your partner isn't open to change and doesn't respect your views and opinions. You can't agree to disagree with each other and tries to prove the other wrong no matter what. If you find yourself spending more time fighting with your partner than being happy, you clearly are mismatched.

7. Different outlooks on the future:

Two people may be in the same relationship, but they rarely are on the same page. While one might be thinking about getting engaged or married soon, the other might flee to the hills just at the mere name of commitment. One might talk about having kids one day while the other just brushes off the idea that they're not ready for that yet. One must be thinking about traveling the world while the other just wants to stay peacefully in the town. It's best to start talking about your future early in the relationship to see where both of you stand in each other's lives.

Conclusion:

The signs mentioned above are all the major red flags of incompatibility. But, in addition, you must have a sense of mutual respect, understanding, and effort with your partner. For example, suppose you feel that the relationship is one-sided, with you giving your all, making sacrifices, trying to be consistent with them. Yet, at the same time, they couldn't care less about you and don't appreciate or value all that you do for them. In that case, you should consider moving out of the relationship for good.

www.ingramcontent.com/pod-product-compliance
Lightning Source LLC
Chambersburg PA
CBHW070923080526
44589CB00013B/1408